WORKING MOTHERS INSPIRING OTHERS

THE SECRET TO MAKING IT WORK

SARAH MACONACHIE

Copyright © Sarah Maconachie
First published in Australia in 2024
by KMD Books
Waikiki, WA 6169

All rights reserved. No part of this book may be used or reproduced by any means, graphic, electronic, or mechanical, including photocopying, recording, taping or by any information storage retrieval system without the written permission of the copyright owner except in the case of brief quotations embodied in critical articles and reviews.

Because of the dynamic nature of the Internet, any web addresses or links contained in this book may have changed since publication and may no longer be vaild. The views expressed in this work are solely those of the author and do not necessarily reflect the views of the publisher and the publisher hereby disclaims any responsibility for them.

Edited by Hannah Lawrence
Interior design by Dylan Ingram
Proofread by Gill Hunter
Cover design by Dylan Ingram

National Library of Australia Catalogue-in-Publication data:
Working Mothers Inspiring Others/Sarah Maconachie

ISBN:
978-0-9925884-6-5
(Hardback)

ISBN:
978-0-9925884-3-4
(Paperback)

ISBN:
978-0-9925884-2-7
(Ebook)

DEDICATION

To all the incredible mothers out there juggling lives that no longer belong solely to you. To the mothers who became mothers against all odds. To the mothers who want to work, need to work, and those who stay at home.

To all the incredible mothers out there, this book is for you.

I think most will agree that being a mother is the best and most challenging role we will ever have. From the moment we become pregnant, our babies become our number one priority, and we embark on a journey that pushes us to our limits, creates feelings we have never experienced before, and changes our entire world.

When our babies arrive, we have a beautiful newborn whose needs we tend to every minute of every day. We are trying to recover from nine months of growing them and then giving birth, and let's face it, there is no easy way to get a baby out! Our bodies are incredible, and as mothers, we are too. This book is here to support any woman who has endured the postpartum pain, the exhaustion of raising a family, the identity shift, and the career change because her needs no longer seem to matter compared to the new life that has entered the world.

Mothers come from all walks of life. There are mothers who have faced various challenges in life and encountered different challenges since becoming a parent. There is no right or wrong when it comes to being a mother. This book hears, supports, and applauds all the mothers who follow their heart, challenge the status quo, and push through this incredible journey we call motherhood.

To the employers paving the way for balanced and flexible working arrangements, making it possible for more mothers to return to work, this book commends you. And to the businesses that have yet to offer such arrangements, let this book inspire you.

To all the women out there, you are doing an incredible job, no matter what your journey is and whatever your path may be.

With love from all the wonderful mothers who have shared their journeys in our book and the author who brought it all together.

CONTENTS

INTRODUCTION	1
SARAH MACONACHIE	3
VICKY WREN	13
TRACEY VERMAAK	29
STACEY WEBB	39
CHERYL EDWARDES – INTERVIEW	49
TANIA GOMEZ	61
SARAH COLEMAN	71
KERRY McNAMEE	79
CARLA LOMBARDO	91
LISA YOUNGER – INTERVIEW	105
ASHLEY McGRATH	117
NICOLA VEAL	127
LEISA VAN GEEST	139
FIONA YUE	151
KATE O'HARA – INTERVIEW	159
SANDRA LEE	171
ALICIA WHITE	181
MICHELLE TRAVIS	193
ABOUT SARAH MACONACHIE	203
CONCLUSION	205
WORKSHEETS	207

ACKNOWLEDGE
MEET THE AUTHORS

SARAH MACONACHIE
WORK HARD PARENT HARD

VICKY WREN
VICTORIA WREN CONSULTING

TRACEY VERMAAK
WA SETTLEMENT SERVICES

STACEY WEBB
STACEY WEBB

ACKNOWLEDGE
MEET THE AUTHORS

CHERYL EDWARDES
HONORARY SPECIAL COUNCIL
AND CHAIR

TANIA GOMEZ
STRAWBERRY SOLUTIONS &
TANIA GOMEZ CONSULTING

SARAH COLEMAN
CEO IDOBA

KERRY MCNAMEE
HUMAN RESOURCES

ACKNOWLEDGE
MEET THE AUTHORS

CARLA LOMBARDO
EAGLE & OWL

LISA YOUNGER
EVOLVING DOORS

ASHLEY MCGRATH
CEOS FOR GENDER EQUITY

NICOLA VEAL
HUMAN RESOURCES

ACKNOWLEDGE
MEET THE AUTHORS

LEISA VAN GEEST
BANKING

FIONA YUE
PGY CONSULTANTS & MERINO AND CO

KATE O'HARA
FOODBANK

SANDRA LEE
THE EMPOWERMENT ADVENTURE

ACKNOWLEDGE
MEET THE AUTHORS

ALICIA WHITE
ACTION & EMERGENCY PTY LTD

MICHELLE TRAVIS
UNIVERSITY OF SAN FRANCISCO SCHOOL OF LAW

INTRODUCTION

We are here to acknowledge, admire, and celebrate all the incredible things that mothers do. If raising our children, cooking, cleaning, washing, and everything else that goes into running a household isn't enough, many of us also add a career into the mix.

We are incredible human beings, and this book has been created to shake things up, speak openly and honestly about what it's like to be a working mother, and provide support to all the other amazing mothers out there. This collection of stories will make you laugh, cry, inspire you, challenge you, and instil a determination in you to chase your dreams and create a life that you love.

Whatever your own situation is, you will find a story in this book you can relate to. Get ready for an inspiring journey as we delve into the incredible stories of 18 fearless working mothers. From a lawyer having her documents delivered to her via a taxi in the 1980s so she could work from home, to mums who had plans to stay at home but decided it wasn't for them, to the entrepreneurs creating more than just magic at home. The careers these incredible women have chosen often have their children at the forefront of their minds. They share how they made it work, how they created balance, and how they integrated work and parenting as one.

As you dive into these stories, you will hear from mothers who had the courage to ask for help and acknowledge when they needed it. You'll read about mothers who faced health concerns and serious illnesses and how these experiences shaped their journeys and perspectives in life. You'll discover the courageous women who bravely spoke up to their employers to ensure the flexibility they needed was provided in the workplace, and what those conversations looked like.

This book is a call to action, urging mothers to create a life they love, work when they want to, and follow their dreams. The chapters in this book are here to guide you on a beautiful journey of self-discovery, empowerment, and motherhood—a journey over which you have complete control. At the end of this book, you'll find a set of worksheets designed to challenge your current situation and help you pave your path forward. Your confidence, mindset, and desires are crucial as a mother. It's time to discover what you truly want, your purpose, what makes you happy, and create a life as a working mother centred around that. We have complete control over our destinies, and it's up to YOU to choose the path for your life and your children's lives.

A happy mother creates happy children, so turn the page and embark on the incredibly inspiring journeys of the working mothers in this book. The advice and wisdom you encounter could change your life forever.

SARAH MACONACHIE

> MY PRIORITY HAS BECOME MYSELF. I DO WHAT I NEED TO EASE MY OWN GUILT, MAKE MYSELF FEEL MENTALLY HEALTHY, AND CREATE THE BALANCE I NEED TO FUNCTION AT MY BEST.

Sarah has three young children, the eldest being four, and two-year-old twins. After a year at home with the twins, like many other mothers, Sarah felt lost, lacking in purpose and confidence. After a successful career in recruitment, Sarah decided it was time to pursue something she was passionate about and became the director of a mindset consultancy – PGY Consultants. Sarah is the author of two books and a co-author of another, she has her own blog and business, 'Work Hard Parent Hard,' where Sarah helps parents to change their mindsets, regain their purpose and drive as a working parent and transform their lives.

SARAH MACONACHIE

AUTHOR NAME: SARAH MACONACHIE
BUSINESS NAME: WORK HARD PARENT HARD
POSITION: FOUNDER | DIRECTOR
BUSINESS INDUSTRY: MINDSET CONSULTING
WEBSITE: WWW.WORKHARDPARENTHARD.COM.AU
INSTAGRAM: @WORKHARDPARENTHARD
FACEBOOK: FACEBOOK.COM/WORKHARDPARENTHARD
LINKEDIN: LINKEDIN.COM/IN/SARAH-MACONACHIE-18BA9B85

My childhood, in a word, was wonderful. I was extremely lucky to be raised in a very equal household where my parents were both involved in parenting me and my two sisters. My dad was a teacher, and my mum ran her own daycare centre. Everyone was home by 4:15pm, family dinner was at 5:15pm, and we spent a lot of time together. During the holidays, my dad would have us for half of the holidays by himself while Mum worked. We went on the most magical adventures (so we thought!) which ranged from a trip to the tip, to helping him find rogue golf balls for when he played golf. When he played squash, he would assign us tasks to create something for him. We always had the BEST time, and he had a brilliant way of making every activity so much fun. For the second half of the holidays, Mum would also take time off, and we would go on family holidays and do things together. Although a lot of the fun memories are from times with Dad, I was also very close with my mum. As a child, I was often referred to as her 'shadow' because I never left her side. I would often get home from school and sit at the dinner table just talking to Mum while she cooked dinner, and offering help when I could. I always felt incredibly loved and supported by both my parents.

When I was seven, my dad was sick and was off work for an extended period of time. Luckily, my mum had her business, but I remember us having to watch what we spent and cut back on things. During that time, we stopped horse riding on Sundays, but my sisters and I didn't mind! All three of us just wanted to do what we could to support Mum and Dad during difficult times. This created a real need to be independent myself. I moved to Australia from England when I was 22 and always strived to be completely self-sufficient and internally happy. At the age of 26, I moved into an apartment by myself and absolutely loved it. I felt completely independent and totally self-sufficient—something I had always wanted. And then boom! Along came my husband. It's funny how the world works at times.

When it was time to start my own family, I knew I wanted to create a similar upbringing to the one I had myself. My sisters and I have all married men who have been hands-on parents, sharing the load. I thank my parents for being such great role models; they have shaped three daughters who are career-driven and loving mothers with partners who reflect the same.

My sisters and I all moved out of home when we were 18. While I moved to Australia, my sisters moved to London, which is just a few hours from my parents. We have always lived free-spirited, independent lives. We were always encouraged to pursue our desires in life and were taught that we can achieve anything we set our minds to. It's that attitude that has brought me to where I am today. We had boundaries, respect, and a lot of love in our house, and I will be forever grateful for my parents, who taught me so much and allowed me to have the freedom that I desired so desperately while growing up.

When my first baby Sofia was born, it was perfect. My parents were here, my husband's parents were here, and my sister came to visit shortly after with her husband and their two children. We had the most magical time with everyone.

Being a mum came quite naturally to me, and I was extremely lucky to have a baby that was easy. She had reflux, and I may have smelled like vomit permanently, but apart from that, she was wonderful!

Sofia was all about Mummy. She wanted me all the time, and I felt quite strongly about supporting her views (as a nine-month-old baby, haha!). When I was being pressured to give her to someone else and just let her scream, I would push back and say, "Why don't you sit next to us and play with her that way?" I didn't see the point in distressing my child just because others thought I should. I am so glad I stuck to my guns. She has grown up to be secure, independent, and still as wilful as she was as a baby.

I returned to work when Sofia was 11 months old, working three days a week in the city doing recruitment. It was about a 50% pay decrease from what I was earning before, but I wanted something easy, something that wasn't super challenging. I felt like I wanted to focus on my children, and thus couldn't have it all. I felt I had to compromise my abilities and self-worth in order to be a working parent—something I cringe at when I look back.

I would drop my daughter off at daycare and get to work early. I have always been a morning person; it's when I get all my good work done. So, I was hoping I would be able to leave a bit earlier to pick up Sofia at a reasonable time. With support from my manager, I started leaving at 4:00pm after working my 8-hour day. But after a while, my manager advised me that other line managers and staff members were "watching" us, and I couldn't really leave early to pick up my daughter (even though I got to work early to make up the time). I hated it. I would get this pang of guilt come 4:00pm, and I desperately wanted to pick her up. Her educators always mentioned she would get antsy at 4:00pm-ish and start to want Mummy. They would laugh at how she seemed to know the exact time, which, for me, meant the exact time she'd had enough and needed to come home.

For a period of time, I picked her up at about 5:15pm, if I was lucky. She would be so tired and grumpy, she wouldn't eat anything, would throw her food around, and then it was bath time and straight to bed. I felt awful. I got no time with her in the evenings, and I felt like that 4:00pm guilt just wasn't worth it.

Just as I'd had enough, COVID struck, and we were all asked to work from home. It was GREAT. My husband and I were both working from home, and everything felt so much easier.

We dropped Sofia off at daycare around 8:00am and picked her up at 4:00pm. We soon realised how lovely it was having that balance, and most importantly, having her dad home. Their relationship went from strength to strength during this time, and it was the most wonderful thing to witness.

It was during this time that our ways of parenting shifted. We became more equal and started sharing the load of caring for Sofia. Thankfully, she was becoming quite the daddy's girl—right on time for me to fall pregnant with twins!

We were in our little bubble! Then we were told we had to return to the office full-time. Due to being pregnant with twins, I had horrendous nausea. I would get up in the morning and almost cry at the thought of having to push myself through the next eight or so hours before I could be back home. At work, I would sit at my desk with a loaf of bread and some dry crackers, willing myself to eat because I felt hungry, but then trying not to vomit after eating. My anxiety was horrendous. I decided during this time that I wanted (and needed) to do something that involved me working from home.

I was about seven weeks pregnant and in the peak of feeling really awful when I got a new job as the Business and Workforce Manager at a Labour Hire Company. It was fun, new, and completely flexible! I went up to four days a week, knowing that I wanted to have extra money in savings when the twins arrived.

The flexibility during my pregnancy was so important. As I was having twins, I had regular check-ups, extra appointments, and an extra-large bump to navigate. I finished working at 30 weeks pregnant. It was Christmas time, and I got to the point where I couldn't get around anymore. I was tired, sore, and starting to struggle. We got through Christmas, and then I ended up on bedrest for four (very long) days before the twins made their grand entrance into the world on the 26th of January 2021.

The newborn phase is quite a blur, or maybe I've repressed it—who knows! My husband and I soon realised we needed to both be hands-on to make it work. He took six (short) weeks off from work to help me, and then I was on my own with three kids under 2 years old… Shit! As the twins were premature, they were on 3-4 hourly feeds for what felt like forever. I was so exhausted that my husband would often get up in the night to feed them and let me catch up on some sleep. I still, to this day, have no idea how he did it and worked all day, but teamwork makes the dream work! And we really did well in that first six months of being parents to twins.

I stopped breastfeeding after five months. I was expressing 1.5 litres of milk a day—and boy oh boy, was my body feeling it. I was exhausted, and I was getting awful heart palpitations to the point where I ended up in the Emergency room. After a number of tests, the doctors put it down to my body just doing way too much. I decided it was time to cut off the supply! I was never precious about whether to breastfeed or not, and I have always thought that a healthy me is the best thing for my children. So, I started weaning them off, and I was done.

When the twins were around 6-12 months, I felt like I had hit rock bottom. They were constantly sick, my hormones were a mess, and I was trying all sorts to regulate them. I felt anxious, depressed, and like I was completely losing my mind. I was diagnosed with Premenstrual Dysphoric Disorder (PMDD) and started on antidepressants to try and balance out the "hormonal hangover" I had gone into. I was persistent and determined with doctors. I knew I wasn't myself; I wasn't responding to things the way I knew I usually would, and this self-awareness really helped me realise that I needed support. To top it all off, my parents couldn't come to see us and help due to COVID and there were many calls to my mum in desperation to see her and have some help. It was really hard.

Twelve months after the twins were born, I returned to work two days a week. I had no idea how I was going to do it. I was not feeling like myself; I was exhausted, I had lost all my confidence, and I had no idea how I was going to make it work. My baby brain was awful; I was foggy, my memory was terrible, I couldn't think of what I wanted to say. I felt like I had lost all my intelligence. But I also knew that I couldn't stay at home with three young children and that I needed something for me to try and rebuild myself.

So, I returned to work from home two days a week. My medication started kicking in, and my confidence started coming back. The twins were settled in daycare, and I decided after a few months—and a long-awaited trip to the UK to see my family—that it was time for change. I was ready for a fresh start.

I wrote down a list of exactly what I wanted and needed to make it work. I wanted three days a week, flexibility, and to be in a role I really enjoyed. I wanted to be stimulated again and to be exercising my brain—I needed it!

This is when I met Fiona, the founder of PGY Consultants, and my life took a big turn for the better.

I quickly joined the program PGY Consultants offered, knowing that I needed to make some changes, and went on an incredible mindset journey. It took time and it took some hard work, but I found my drive, motivation, and, most importantly, my purpose. I felt like I found a piece of myself that had been missing since I had children, and I could see hints of the former me. With time, I grew to accept and love the "new me." I'm still the driven and ambitious person I always was, but now with three children in tow. I have realised there is a way to balance both being a working mum and being fully present for my children. And I have minimal guilt. Yes, I would love to spend more time at work, but the gratitude I have for being with my children on my days off overrides that, and I accept that this period of my life requires a juggle and some patience toward my job and my children.

I now work completely flexible hours. If I need to do school drop-off, I do it; if I need to leave early to pick someone up, I do. The love I have for my job means I am happy to work more and go above and beyond when I need to, and in return, I work flexibly to fit in around the needs of my children. I feel so lucky to be working in a job I love and to have a blend of work and being a mother that makes me feel guilt-free, empowered, and, most importantly, happy.

My confidence to communicate what I need with work and at home has been my greatest asset. I was upfront and honest before I started my role at PGY Consultants; I wanted everything agreed to in writing prior to starting so I could work around the needs of my children and prevent that awful 4:00pm feeling when I desperately want to leave to get my kids. The same goes at home. My husband isn't psychic, and he also doesn't think in the same way I do as a mother. I soon learned that my expectations needed to change with him. I can't just assume he knows what I want him to do to help with the children and around the house. So, I started discussing what I needed him to do. Luckily for me, he is incredibly good around the house anyway, and he is now a very efficient dad and takes on 50% of the responsibilities. I rarely have to ask him, and I absolutely love the relationships he has developed with our children by being so hands-on. As women and mothers, we sometimes need to offer support to our partners and educate them about what we need them to do to support us.

My priority has become myself. I do what I need to ease my own guilt, make myself feel mentally healthy, and create the balance I need to function at my best. Knowing what my children need is essential, and working around that becomes my number one priority because it prevents my guilt and discomfort as a working mother. I can see my children's behaviour and mood mirroring my own, and I understand how important it is to be happy in myself. By prioritising myself a bit more, I am doing a better job all over. It's hard as a mother to put yourself first, but it is so worth it!

Going through my mindset journey has allowed me to regain my purpose and make myself a priority again. It has given me the confidence to go out on my own and focus completely on my own business, "Work Hard Parent Hard." I am forever grateful for the journey I went on with my own mindset, and now, I focus on helping other parents go on the same journey. It has enabled me to understand my children and my husband a million times better, and I wish every mum (and dad) could feel the way I do.

My advice to all the working mothers out there is to understand what you need to feel happy. Communicate what that looks like to those who need to know and keep communicating to make sure it remains. A happy mother is the best thing you can do for your children, and let's face it, life's too incredible and way too short to not love the life that you are living!

VICKY WREN

> AS I'VE WORKED THROUGH WHAT I REALLY WANT, THE TRICKIEST PART HAS BEEN DIFFERENTIATING BETWEEN WHAT I THOUGHT I 'SHOULD' WANT AND WHAT I TRULY 'DO' WANT. THIS PROCESS OF SELF-DEVELOPMENT AND DISCOVERY HAS SPANNED OVER MORE THAN A DECADE, LEADING ME TO WHERE I AM NOW.

Vicky, an accountant with over two decades of experience, brings a unique and contagious energy to her work. She is passionate about everything she throws herself into and her genuine enthusiasm, coupled with an optimistic outlook on life, uplifts those around her. She has a knack for recognising and cultivating the raw potential in others, which has resulted in her developing a number of high-performing teams. Her 'bread and butter' is in developing and operationalising processes and systems to support data-backed decision-making, but as an idea's person who thrives on building relationships, problem-solving by connecting the dots others don't always see, is her real jam.

VICKY WREN

AUTHOR NAME: VICKY WREN
BUSINESS NAME: VICKY WREN CONSULTING
POSITION: FOUNDER
BUSINESS INDUSTRY: LEADERSHIP DEVELOPMENT & BUSINESS CONSULTING
WEBSITE: WWW.VICKYWRENCONSULTING.COM
LINKEDIN: LINKEDIN.COM/IN/VICKY-WREN-19941A43

WHAT TYPE OF MUM ARE YOU?

I love to chat, and my openness to talk about real stuff means that I often dive straight into deep and meaningful conversations, especially with other mums. Over the years, I have come across common themes of mums not feeling like they are enough, especially when it comes to their work choices and a deep sense of overwhelm with the juggle and mental load of parenting. Whilst we have the most choice career-wise of any previous generations, this comes with huge pressure to 'be it all'.

To assist in identifying what type of mother you are, I have made some broad generalisations. My intention is to specifically address work, both paid and unpaid, without diminishing the uniqueness we all possess as individuals. I believe that identifying with one of these types, whether it's innate or due to a stage in life, will help alleviate some of the pressure we feel to live up to unachievable standards—standards either set by ourselves due to our own internal ideals of perfection or by societal norms.

The four broad categories are:
- 'Career-driven mum'
- 'Job-to-pay-the-bills mum'
- 'Job-to-fit-my-lifestyle mum'
- 'Stay-at-home mum'.

In my conversations over the years, 'career-driven mums' often express guilt for prioritising work or are stretched so thin attempting to balance the competing devotions of career and motherhood. 'Job-to-pay-the-bills mums' and 'job-to-fit-my-lifestyle mums' either stick with uninspiring work, which doesn't fully utilise their skills, to protect their job flexibility, or they may squeeze full-time work into part-time hours but take the pay cut for the flexibility to be with their children more. 'Stay-at-home mums' often express a sense of inadequacy in not earning any money, or "just" looking after the kids. They are usually the ones to say to working mums, "I just don't know how you do it all."

I know that I am a 'career-driven mum', but it has taken me a long time to get comfortable that I can be a great mum and be passionate about my work without driving myself to burnout to achieve both. As I've worked through what I really want, the trickiest part has been differentiating between what I thought I 'should' want and what I truly 'do' want. This process of self-development and discovery has spanned across more than a decade, leading me to where I am now.

WHAT WILL YOU TAKE AWAY?
As you read my story, my hope is that you will reflect on the type of mum you are and get comfortable with owning it, letting go of the pressure to be something else. However, if, like many mums, you're stuck on the hamster wheel and haven't had a spare minute to think about what you want or who you are at an identity level now that you are a mum, my wish is that this might provide you with some ideas on where to start. By reading about some of

the struggles I've had, you may realise that if you feel the same, you are not alone. I believe the answers are within, and only you can understand what's right for you. However, as I've learned, it takes time to rediscover yourself, especially when caring for young children, so give yourself grace—it's a journey.

Disclaimer: this is my story of how motherhood impacted my identity and career, it doesn't take away from my love of being a mother and how much I adore my children. Dr Alexandra Saks sums this up so well in this quote: "Ambivalence is a feeling that comes up in the roles and relationships you're most invested in, because they're always a juggling act between giving and taking. Most of the time, the experience of motherhood is not good or bad, it's both good and bad."

WHERE I'M AT NOW.
I am currently 41 years old, married, and have three children aged 13, 9, and 6. I was born and raised in Zimbabwe, lived in the UK for 12 years where I had my first two children, and now I'm fortunate enough to call Australia my home, and this is where my third child was born. I'm an accountant by trade, and although I love a good Excel formula, my true passion is in developing others by helping them to recognise and cultivate their own raw potential. Most people who meet me would agree that I'm not your stereotypical accountant; I'm an ideas person who loves problem-solving and building meaningful connections and relationships. At the time of writing this chapter, I'm at a crossroads in my career, deciding what's next—so stay tuned for updates!

MY CHILDHOOD AND THE SUBTLE, IMPRINTING MESSAGES I HEARD.
I am one of three children, with an older brother and younger sister. Growing up, my dad worked in the mining industry and travelled a lot, and my mum worked as a math teacher. Being raised in Zimbabwe, I didn't have the stereotypical upbringing that

is often seen in the UK and Australia. We had a maid we called Gogo, which means Granny in Ndebele. She was like a mother to us, doing all the cooking, cleaning, laundry, bathing, and, if we misbehaved, even giving us a smack. She loved us like her own, even though she earned minimum wage and left her own family to live on our property as part of the job. This meant that the cooking, cleaning, laundry, and the notion of 'not being able to do a wee in peace' were not things I had ever really thought about as part of a mother's role.

From a young age, I was always told what a great mother I would make. These comments made me want to become a teacher, however, moving into my teen years as a fierce feminist, I decided that teaching was most definitely not what I wanted, primarily due to its low pay in Zimbabwe. I aspired to be an "independent financial woman, who never needed to rely on a man." My feminism and passion for addressing any injustice earned me the nickname Vicious Vick from my dad. I hadn't thought much about why I was such a feminist during my teens, but upon reflection I realised it was because I saw a significant power imbalance between men and women in Zimbabwe driven by financial disparities.

My career choice and the strong themes of independence that influenced it.

In my final years of high school, I entered an accelerated program studying accounting, allowing me to complete four years of study for O and then A-Levels in just two years. I was deeply inspired by my accounting teacher, one of the first 10 females to qualify as an accountant in Zimbabwe, which led me to choose accounting as my career path. I believed that an accounting qualification would grant me the financial freedom to be independent and provide a solid foundation for considering my future career choices. Ironically, my accounting teacher had shifted from practicing as an accountant to teaching to better balance work and her four children!

Choosing accounting as a career was also a way for me to

obtain a degree and an accounting qualification without relying on financial assistance. In Zimbabwe, the 'Big Four' accounting firms offered a five-year training contract to complete accounting articles where they covered the costs of your degree and Chartered Accountant qualification while you worked. Since there were no student loans available and my parents were already paying for my older brother's university, having moved to Zambia to earn US dollars to enable this, I decided not to add any additional financial strain to them. I was determined to take matters into my own hands. This option would lead to me becoming fully qualified by the time I was 23, which was perfect! I didn't want to waste any time climbing the corporate ladder, and I could achieve it all independently without anyone's help. So at aged 18, I started my career in external audit at one of the Big Four accounting firms.

Due to political and economic instability in Zimbabwe, I moved to the UK and ended up completing my degree and accounting qualification in London. By the age of 27, I was offered the role of Finance Director at a global fashion retail company in London. I was already acting in that role when I received the offer, but I had just found out I was nine weeks pregnant with my first child. I turned down the offer, citing "lack of experience" as the reason, but in reality it was because I couldn't reconcile how to be a "good mother" while managing a demanding, high-pressure career. The prevailing narrative in Zimbabwe while I was growing up was, "Why have children if you're not going to raise them yourself?"

NO MOTHERHOOD QUALIFICATIONS.
After enduring 37 hours of labour, our baby girl finally made her entrance into this world. The very next day, we were discharged to go home. I vividly recall my wonderful husband having to pull the car over on the side of the road as we drove home because he was overwhelmed with emotions about our precious baby in the back seat. At that moment, I couldn't help but think, "Hang on, I studied for years to become an accountant, but I've just been sent

home with this tiny little baby, and I don't have a qualification in motherhood!" This theme persisted throughout my journey as a mother.

During my time in the UK, after enduring many sleepless nights trying to get my daughter to settle, I would often wake up later in the morning only to find an Amazon delivery on my doorstep. It was another parenting book that I had ordered during one of my zombie-like, sleep-deprived states in an attempt to get 'qualified' in this mothering thing. I don't think I ever got around to reading any of them, but they were incredibly helpful for propping up my daughter's cot to alleviate her reflux! Not trusting my instincts or thinking that someone else held all the answers continued throughout the next decade.

THE SHOCK OF LONELINESS AND LOSS OF IDENTITY.
That first year on maternity leave was a significant shift from the fast-paced life I had in London. We had moved to a new area (Kent) just three weeks before my due date to buy the "traditional" family home. My closest friend lived in the area, and it was picture-perfect with front gardens meticulously maintained, white picket fences, and a cricket pitch right across the street. It seemed like the ideal place to start the Wren family, even though it meant a challenging daily commute into London—on a good day and if we timed the trains right, it was a minimum three-hour daily commute.

During the first few months of my maternity leave, I felt incredibly lonely. While my bestie lived just a short stroll down the road, she worked during the week. While on the outside I appeared confident, internally I was struggling. I constantly sought external validation and grappled with feelings of loneliness and a loss of identity. I internalised all of this because I believed I was supposed to be this amazing mother who loved every moment of it. In reality, I longed to return to work where I felt valuable and in control.

My daughter was 10 months old when I returned to work. I stayed in the job I loved for a year before it got too hard. I felt like

I was failing my daughter because I wasn't spending the time with her that I wanted due to the London commute. As a result, I took a rare local job—it came with a 50% pay cut. Three years later, despite my misgivings about the mother juggle, we had our second child—a son. I longed for this period of maternity leave because it was an escape from an unhappy and toxic work environment.

I couldn't go back to work in the city with two small dependents, and there were no other local jobs suitable. I felt trapped. I was in a lower paid job so I could focus on my children, because that's what "good mothers" do, right?

The decision to move across the world with two young children and no family support.

I have always been a career-driven and focused woman. While I always wanted children, I didn't realise how much I would miss being the career-driven person I was before having them. Balancing both roles was, and is, challenging.

When my son was eight weeks old, we came to Australia on a holiday to see if we wanted to move here. We emigrated seven months later while I was still on maternity leave. My husband had always wanted to come to Australia, and while I could see it looked like a beautiful place, it was so far away from everyone! Living in our picture-perfect village in Kent, we had built an incredible community around us, and as a person who thrives on connection, leaving was the hardest thing I have ever done. I wanted it all—to live in the perfect family village but also to maintain my career—and this was not going to be possible with the London commute.

When we arrived in Perth, we were extremely lucky to reconnect with two families who we knew from Zimbabwe, and they very much took us under their wings and became our Perth family. When my son was 14 months old and I had settled my daughter into her new school, I returned to the workforce. However, being new to Perth and not having 'Perth experience' made it challenging to find a suitable role, even though I had an impressive CV. In the end, given my domestic juggle, I took a junior role that I was overqualified for. It was less pay, but in my mind that meant less responsibility and I could spend more time with my family. However, I still worked full-time and often worked long hours because I constantly took on projects that were out of the scope of my role to keep myself engaged and stimulated.

With no family support in Perth, we were going to have to share the juggle of drop-offs and pick-ups for school and daycare. Daycare was always relatively easy as they operated for normal business hours; however, now that our daughter was starting school, this was a whole new ball game with later drop-offs and earlier pick-ups. How were we going to manage? My husband and I decided that we would share this responsibility with one of us going in to work early to then be able to do the pick-ups and the other working late so they could do the morning drop-offs. However, workplace flexibility was not what it is post-COVID and this was not going to be option. Since there wasn't any before or after-school care at the school, we found a wonderful nursing student who could help us, albeit a more expensive option. I had major feelings of guilt because I wanted to work, and I wasn't going to be at the school gates every day to fetch my daughter, which seemed the norm, and having a nanny do this was unheard of at her school. I felt like I had prioritised work over family, and this feeling was heightened because the demographics at her school were mainly these amazing stay-at-home mums who prepared beautiful, Instagram-worthy home-cooked lunchbox meals and made their own book week costumes. My overwhelming feelings of being an inadequate and selfish mum who wanted to work led me to throw myself into more work to dull these emotions.

Becoming a mother of three when I still didn't feel like a "good enough" mother.

After a few years of being settled in Perth, I suddenly started to feel this debilitating exhaustion. I assumed it was just the effects of the work and home juggle and my body adjusting to the hormones from the Mirena contraceptive device. One day, driving home from work, my husband said to me, "You aren't pregnant, are you?" I immediately replied, "Of course not," but it hit me like a ton of bricks. Of course, I knew what this tiredness was—I knew this feeling all too well—that early pregnancy tiredness is like no other. This time I wasn't mentally prepared, and how could it be when I was on contraception?! For the next two weeks, I walked to the chemist on my lunch break every day to buy a pregnancy test and walked out again empty-handed. Eventually, I finally did a pregnancy test, and yep, it sure was positive. The next couple of months were an incredibly emotional time. I was trying to get to grips with having a third child when I already felt so inadequate as a mother. At the same time, I was informed that the likelihood of the pregnancy reaching full term was slim, and complications were likely. Despite the odds, my perfectly healthy miracle baby boy was born in March 2017 and has been a source of immense joy. After fighting his way into this world, he is still a force to be reckoned with!

CHOOSING A NEW MOTHERHOOD EXPERIENCE IS POSSIBLE.
This maternity leave was different, I really wanted to enjoy it and not wish it away. Although I still felt lost and didn't know who I was since becoming a mother, during this time I did a lot of self-development. I joined an amazing Mums-only fitness group and started a group coaching program for mums. I listened to audiobooks and devoured free resources. This helped me verbalise and put language around what I was feeling, and seeing so many women in a similar position gave me the reassurance that I wasn't alone. However, I was still very much looking for someone else to tell me what I should want. I remember the first time I splashed out on a 1:1 career coach, I was initially really frustrated that I had paid all this money and she was asking me to tell her what the answers were. I wanted her to just tell me what career I should be doing because motherhood and accounting clearly weren't compatible! It took time for me to really understand that someone else couldn't

give me the answers but could merely hold up the mirror for me, reflecting back what I was saying I actually wanted.

In 2020, three weeks before the whole world changed with COVID, I walked out of my job with nowhere to go to. I was feeling both unfulfilled and burnt out, and at the time I was doing some personal development work with Lisa Corduff all about radical responsibility. I realised that if I wasn't happy then it was up to me and only me to make a change. In this time out of the paid workforce, I discovered Amy Taylor-Kabbaz and spent 12 months studying the identity shift that occurs when you become a mother. It has a name; it's called Matrescence (like adolescence) – it's fascinating. I'd need a whole book to go into the details of it here, but I would highly recommend you go look up Amy. I couldn't believe the power of simply putting language around so many of the feelings I had trying to understand during the motherhood identity shift. I love being a mum to my beautiful children, but I struggled so much with that identity shift of "who am I now?" Over the last few years, I have continued to invest in myself with self-development programs and a personal coach.

REDISCOVERING IS A PROCESS.
It's been a long journey of self-discovery, and I still didn't get it right straight away. With my newfound confidence, post-understanding the motherhood identity shift and realising that I wasn't 'broken,' I decided that I was no longer going to do a job that was well below my abilities, and one that was part-time so I didn't burn myself out again. I thought working part-time was the answer. In my most recent role in an incredible organisation, I remember so vividly in the interview when asking about working part-time, my future boss said, "I believe an organisation should work for the individual, not the other way around." His premise was that we'll design the work around you – you just tell us what you want. This organisation has had the most profound impact on me, from the incredible people I have worked with to an inspirational CEO

who actively encourages you to be your 'true authentic self' and believes that diversity of thought should be celebrated. I'm not sure I ever really knew who my 'true authentic self' was, but I sure am discovering her now.

Through this discovery process I realised that I do think differently to those around me, particularly in the very black-and-white world of accounting—but that's not a bad thing! This made so much sense when I was diagnosed with ADHD earlier this year, which was incredibly validating. It has helped me understand why my mind is always going a million miles an hour and my need to constantly solve problems and "connect the dots." While I know that this has very much been my superpower in my career, it has given me the grace to forgive myself for some of the downfalls I have felt as a mother—my inability to do a simple meal plan, the chaos in the house I just can't get on top of, the lack of routine, constantly being late... These were all things that completely overwhelmed me. My inner mean mama voice, named Gertrude, would shout so loud at me for being such a failure, but now I'm more confident to say, "Thank you, Gertrude, but you can f*ck off. I don't need you anymore."

KNOWING THYSELF AND PUTTING SUPPORT SYSTEMS IN PLACE.
Now understanding how important it is to my happiness to be able to stimulate my mind, I work full-time, and in intrinsically knowing my value, my earnings are finally back up to where they were more than a decade ago. This has enabled me to outsource more, which I couldn't afford to do previously. While a cleaner has always been a necessity in my books (even when living in a sharehouse in London with three stinky boys), I also have a nanny who picks the kids up from school and covers all the kids' laundry. I also have a wonderful local lady who cooks me three fresh meals a week so most weeknight dinners are sorted. The most valuable outsource, however, was having another school mum help me sort out the chaos in the house, where everything now has a home.

She's become a good friend and regularly helps me stay on top of things! This has significantly reduced the overwhelm in the day-to-day running of the home. With the outsourcing, it's something that ebbs and flows for me; when I need the help, I now go out and get it.

PARTING WORDS OF WISDOM.

While the process of self-discovery has been a very long journey for me and may not have come easily, once I started doing the below things, everything changed.

INVEST IN AND PRIORITISE YOURSELF

If you have the financial means, invest in a personal coach; the investment will reap great rewards. If you don't, don't despair! There are so many free resources out there, even starting with podcasts while you cook dinner or hang up a load of laundry is a great place to start.

If you work, don't consider your working hours as 'time off' from the kids, and if you're a stay-at-home mum, don't think that you don't deserve the same 'time off' as other parents – you do work, it's just unpaid! Learning to prioritise myself has taken practice and it changes all the time—and I'm not just talking about taking time off to get my hair cut! At first, 'my time' looked like prioritising an hour at the beach straight after school drop-off, sipping on a delicious coffee and listening to a podcast. Then, I started doing things again that I loved and made me 'me'. I took up ocean swimming and signed up for swimming events that I knew I wasn't fit enough for but did anyway, and it was such a great sense of achievement. It was something I always wanted to do, but I had put it off for so long because I "didn't have the time."

LIVE TO YOUR VALUES, NOT CULTURAL MESSAGING

By understanding yourself and what truly makes you happy, you'll be able to identify your own values. Knowing your values is your

North Star, ensure you live to those and don't sweat everything else, even if society says you should.

OWN WHO YOU WANT TO BE

Whichever category of working mum you have identified with, if you are happy – own it! As a 'stay-at-home mum' you're the goddamn CEO of the household—don't undervalue that! If you have been out of the workplace and are considering returning to work, don't think of that 'gap' in your CV. There is no gap—write the job role of being the CEO of your home! If you're unsure of your strengths, ask those around you in a short text message. This was a valuable exercise I recently learned. Another tool that I'm a big fan of is the CliftonStrengths® assessment which is a performance-based tool that builds self-awareness around your strengths.

If you identify with 'job-to-pay-the-bills mum' but are burning yourself out doing full-time work for part-time pay, once you understand your value and can articulate it, this will open so many opportunities around your financial reward linked to your output, not time at a desk.

If you're in the 'job-to-fit-my-lifestyle mum' category but feel uninspired and underutilised, start by knowing and believing in the value you can bring to an organisation. Get comfortable with communicating your boundaries around work and home, and then seek out opportunities that utilise the skills you have.

And finally, if you in the 'career-driven mums' category, know and accept that motherhood and career-hood are competing devotions. If your career demands more time of you, and you enjoy this, then do it! But look at ways you can outsource the running of the home so that when you are at home this time can be fully dedicated to being present with your family.

It took me an incredibly long time to figure out what I needed, so I hope that this book and its advice helps you to find your true self. Remember that you have the choice to live your life the way you want.

TRACEY VERMAAK

❝ I ENCOURAGE ANYONE WHO IS THINKING ABOUT RE-ENTERING THE WORKFORCE AFTER HAVING CHILDREN TO JUST TAKE THE PLUNGE. TRUST IN YOURSELF, UTILISE YOUR SUPPORT NETWORK, AND YOU WILL FIND IT INCREDIBLY REWARDING. ❞

Tracey is a hands-on mum and a dedicated businesswoman who cherishes a well-balanced life. She is the proud mother of two girls, aged nine and ten. In addition to running her own small business as a real estate settlement agent, she provides essential support to her husband in managing his booming plumbing business. She thrives in a fast-paced, successful environment and places a strong emphasis on maintaining her fitness and overall health, even venturing into bodybuilding over the past two years. Above all, she treasures her supportive husband, her wonderful daughters, who have allowed her to grow and learn, and her incredible circle of friends and colleagues who stand by her with unwavering support and encouragement, free from judgment.

TRACEY VERMAAK

AUTHOR NAME: TRACEY VERMAAK
BUSINESS NAME: WA SETTLEMENT SERVICES
POSITION: DIRECTOR / LICENCED REAL ESTATE SETTLEMENT AGENT
BUSINESS INDUSTRY: REAL ESTATE
WEBSITE: WASETTLEMENTS.COM.AU
LINKEDIN: LINKEDIN.COM/IN/TRACEYVERMAAK
LINKEDIN: LINKEDIN.COM/COMPANY/WA-SETTLEMENT-SERVICES
FACEBOOK: FACEBOOK.COM/WASETTLEMENTSERVICES
INSTAGRAM: @WASETTLEMENTSERVICESAU

Growing up in the 80s, I had a pretty typical childhood. Dad worked, and Mum stayed at home. Dad was the breadwinner, and Mum looked after the house and the kids—myself and my two sisters. Every day, she helped get us ready, packed our (delicious!) lunches, and dropped us off and picked us up from school. Yep, every day. There was no before or after-school care for us—it wasn't even an option where I grew up. She would tend to us after school while preparing dinner. Dad would walk in the door, switch the news on the telly, and come to dinner obediently when called. This was my 'normal' upbringing, well, what I considered to be normal.

As for the 'abnormal' side of my upbringing, I was raised as a Jehovah's Witness due to my mum's religious beliefs.

This made life a bit difficult growing up for a number of reasons.

Firstly, I was targeted at school, constantly teased, and misunderstood. Kids just didn't understand why I couldn't go to their birthday parties, celebrate Easter or Christmas, or even sing the national anthem! To top it off, my sisters and I were the only JW's in the school! Talk about isolation.

Secondly, with this type of upbringing, we were always taught that "Armageddon was just around the corner." For those unfamiliar, this essentially means that the world in which we live in now will be destroyed, along with all the non-believers. The world will then transform into a paradise that only the survivors—the Jehovah's Witnesses—will inhabit and enjoy. We were brought up with the belief that it was highly unlikely we were going to grow up to even reach adult life. Yep, I know what you're thinking. Crazy, right? But it was 100% ingrained in our lives.

Reliving this, the memories came flooding back to me! We were also discouraged, especially as women, to pursue any type of career. And we were strongly encouraged to be a "pioneer of the truth". This, therefore, became my goal and dream for many years during my early to mid-teens, until I left the religion in my early 20s. Please note that I mean no offence to any Jehovah's Witnesses, I believe everyone is entitled to their own beliefs, but it was my time to explore life for myself.

I was about 10 years old when the inkling of being a career woman first came to me. It was a sunny day in the small country town of Crystal Brook, South Australia, and a well-dressed middle-aged man in a suit knocked on our door. This was back when friends and family would pop round just for a chinwag. He wasn't a friend nor family, but he was a salesman. It was either Electrolux or Encyclopedia Britanica, I can't remember which one, but I do distinctively remember the swift movement of this man reaching into his top pocket and whipping out a business card. Coming from a JW family, I had never seen a business card before. "Wow this man is so cool," I thought to myself, "He has a card with his own name on it and he gives it to people. He must be so important!"

From that moment on, all I wanted was to have my own business card. And I was determined to make it happen.

This, of course, was not easy, given that I was not encouraged to go to university or further my education. I had no idea where to start or what to do. I felt like I had nothing. Growing up in such a small country town meant there was little to no work. This, combined with the high unemployment rates of the 80s made it incredibly hard to find a job. So, I started cold calling (visiting) local businesses. I would pop in on a weekly basis and say hi to local business owners to see if any opportunities had opened. This was pretty hard at the time because I was a shy kid, but if I had nothing else, at least I had tenacity.

Finally, when I was a teenager, I was offered a basic office administration job in a fibreglass factory. It was owned by a lovey man called Louis who, many years later, admitted to me that he gave me the job because he felt sorry for me. I don't recall what I said at the interview to make him feel sorry for me, but it worked! I had my first real job! I was in!

I finally had my foot in the door. From there I moved to Adelaide and got into the legal industry as a legal secretary, which was exactly what I wanted to do at the time. I won myself over in this interview due to my lucky ability to touch type at an incredible speed. Now, with some industry experience up my sleeve, I was able to move onwards and upwards quite quickly.

I spent 2002-2005 on an extended working holiday in the UK. It was one of the most treasured experiences of my life! Here I furthered my career working in the legal industry, made lifelong friends, and met my husband Ross, a Zimbabwean on a British passport, who had, at 17 years of age, left Zimbabwe to make a life for himself in England. Ross and I worked mostly in clubs and pubs, gaining some managerial experience working in a pub in Southwest England.

As you can see, my entire career was built from the ground

up, talking my way into roles, working hard, and proving what I was capable of along the way.

In 2005 we moved to Perth, and this is where my career really took shape. I was lucky enough to gain employment with a small family law firm, which is now the largest family law firm in Perth. My boss was (and still is) an amazing woman who encouraged and inspired me. My bold, brilliant, and successful boss was the woman I wanted to learn from, both in business and in life. And that I did! From furthering my education and starting my legal career, to running a business and even giving birth! I have valued every piece of advice from this wonderful woman. In fact, to this day, we remain good friends and often catch up, whether just for a general chat, to reflect on the past, or discuss ideas and plans for the future.

I worked my way up over the next seven and a half years and became the Office Manager while also leading the conveyancing division at the law firm, all thanks to my boss for putting me through my Diploma in Financial Services. It was around this time that I became a mum to my two beautiful daughters, Lillian and Savannah. I had them in quick succession—they are 18 months apart—and just two weeks after giving birth to Lillian, I was back at work full-time, partly at home and partly from the office.

I loved being a working mum. I thrived off juggling the kids and being able to exercise my brain. I was fortunate to work in an office full of amazing women, and a boss that allowed me to bring Lillian in. Thankfully Lillian was a snoozer and slept all day and everyone wanted a cuddle. It was like pass the parcel (read: baby) until she was ready for a feed, then she would be strategically handed back in my direction.

Not long after my second child, to my boss's surprise, I reluctantly handed in my resignation. I was ready to go out on my own. I started up my own settlement agency working from home, and I took a huge amount of pride in finalising the design of my own business cards! My dream was becoming my reality.

However, I hated working from home. There was always the distraction of housework. Did the washing need to be put on? What was I going to make for dinner? Did I need to run to the shop for more milk? Plus, the girls needed to be fed, changed, and entertained. To make matters a little bit more difficult, we had a small house, and I was working from my pool table! That pool table never got as much action than when it served as my "office".

Nope—this just wasn't working for me. I decided I needed to separate work and family life.

An opportunity came up to purchase a small, established settlement agency in Northbridge. This was perfect! A small, affordable office with a landline. No more clients having my mobile number. When I was at work, I could be fully present for my clients. When it at home, I could be solely a mum and a wife.

Being a working mum is so important to me because it keeps my life balanced. I was having a coffee with an employee and good friend of mine the other day who has two young boys and she said, "Trace, the two days a week that I come into work are actually like my days off!" I've heard this so many times over the years and I know that so many working mums can relate to this comment. We go back to work because it's time to breathe, time away from the kids, time to have adult conversations, time to be normal, time to thrive, and our time to be successful. This keeps me, and so many other mums I know, sane.

While it is rewarding, it can also be challenging. You literally feel like you never stop! I'm lucky that I only really work on my business two days a week. The other three days of the working week, I get to be a mum, housewife, and I support my husband with his plumbing business. With my husband's business being our main source of income, I am extremely lucky to have been able to adapt to this wonderful and fulfilling work life balance.

A typical "non-work" day starts with getting up early to walk the dog and tackle the morning chores before the kids wake up. Once they're awake, it's time to make lunches, prepare breakfast, and help the girls with their morning routine before rushing out the door to school. After that, I head to the gym, often followed by a business-related meeting with my husband or an employee. Then, I move on to meal planning, grocery shopping, meal preparation, baking, and housework—fitting in whatever I can before the 3:00pm school pick-up. Depending on the day of the week, we attend swimming, tutoring, netball, or dancing between dinner and showers, making sure to squeeze in homework. By the time I've eaten dinner and the girls are asleep, I'm totally exhausted and ready for bed myself. Finding an hour or so to spend with my husband proves difficult, but it's something we are working on because we know how important it is.

A "workday" looks similar in the morning, except after school drop off, I head straight into work and I utilise after school care so that I can put in a decent day at the office. By the time I pick the girls up and get home, I'm thanking myself for the meal prep I did earlier in the week so we have leftovers. Phew!

I make the most of my travel time to and from work by listening to audiobooks. I alternate between books on business, health, parenting, relationships, and sometimes I just like to get stuck into a good novel. It's either time to grow and learn, or time to enjoy a good story. This time is precious to me. I try to listen to Audible whenever I can, including when I take the dog for a walk or when I go for a long run. Audible + my headphones = my best friends when I'm in need of "me time".

Life is exhausting, mentally and physically. I average 15,000 steps most days, and that's without even trying! But, I love it. I love the balance I have created between being a mum and being a businesswoman—I get the best of both worlds. And I even manage to keep most Fridays free for a "me day". I'll try get a massage, get my hair done, or have lunch with a friend. This work/life balance is truly rewarding, and I really am proud of myself for having found it and being consistent with it.

Certainly, there are many challenges along the way, and I face them daily. My main challenge is not having any family support here in Perth. My mum passed away six years ago, and, in any case, my family is all in South Australia. My husband has a couple of amazing aunts and uncles who I call on when I'm desperate, but I have to say, I'm jealous of those friends of mine (yes, you know who you are) who can call up their mum any day of the week to help out with the kids. And while she's at it, she cleans the entire house, does the washing, puts the slow cooker on, and weeds the garden! Without this support network, we have to outsource, which costs us an arm and a leg in babysitting! Having said this, we do have some truly amazing friends (you also know who you are) who we are able to call on to help us out when things get tough or if we are really stuck.

Parenting challenges alone are huge. Our children are constantly growing, and just when we think we have one issue under control, another one arises. It's a constant battle and we are always needing to learn, adapt, grow as people, and better ourselves. While we are doing this, it's important to remember not to compare ourselves to others or how we were brought up. Our parents had about as much idea as us, which was absolutely no damn clue! We certainly figured out how to make babies and push the little darlings out. Our bodies know how to do this naturally. And parenting is the same. Go with your instinct. My instincts have taught me to parent differently to my mum and dad—no religion, no smacking, and fostering a healthy and balanced approach to life. Oh, and encouraging a career of their own! I know my parents did the very best they could, but it didn't make it right. It took me a few years to learn this, but my number #1 piece of advice is to go with your gut and what you feel is right, not what you were taught or what others do. You know your children better than anyone else. I can honestly say that my dad—and my mum—are so proud of me and the job I am doing raising my children. They 100% respect that I do things differently and haven't once judged or criticised my parenting in any way. In fact, I believe they are secretly amazed at how far we have come as parents and what us mums can achieve these days.

I absolutely love being a busy and successful working mum. Honestly, it's such a joy and it's so fulfilling. I employ four wonderful working mums in my office. Between them, they have children ranging from 1-year-old up to teenagers. I have supported some of these ladies through pregnancy and maternity leave and continue to support them all with a flexible, caring, and understanding working environment so that they too can be happy, successful, and thriving working mums.

I encourage anyone who is thinking about re-entering the workforce after having children to just take the plunge. Trust in yourself, utilise your support network, and you will find it incredibly rewarding. Believe in yourself! Know that you will learn and grow along the way and that you are as capable as anyone else. Talk to your peers, exchange ideas, and don't forget to give yourself a break! We are all human; we make mistakes, and we learn from them. Don't beat yourself up if you make a mistake or take a wrong turn—simply apologise if you need to, learn from it, and move on to become a better person. Life is about learning and growing, and being able to inspire others is super rewarding. Being a working mum keeps me happy, content, and smiling every single day.

STACEY WEBB

> BY NURTURING AND CARING FOR YOUR NERVOUS SYSTEM, YOU EMPOWER YOURSELF TO MEET AND RELEASE LIMITING BELIEFS, FEARS, AND TRAUMAS, ENABLING YOU TO EMBRACE THE JOYS OF PARENTHOOD WHILE EXCELLING IN YOUR PROFESSIONAL ENDEAVOURS.

Stacey Webb is an Intuitive Somatic Mentor and Coach, Trauma-Trained Somatic Practitioner, and a Multi-Award-Winning and Amazon Best-Selling Author. Drawing from a diverse array of expertise spanning trauma, somatics, breathwork, EFT (tapping), intuitive intelligence, metaphysical sciences, and a distinguished 17-year career as a detective within the Police Force, Stacey possesses a unique fusion of skills that elegantly meld the art of healing with profound intuition. This distinctive blend equips her to wholeheartedly support individuals on their transformative healing and awakening journey.

STACEY WEBB

AUTHOR NAME : STACEY WEBB
BUSINESS NAME : STACEY WEBB
POSITION : INTUITIVE SOMATIC MENTOR, COACH, AND AUTHOR
BUSINESS INDUSTRY : WELLNESS AND WELLBEING, MENTORING AND COACHING
WEBSITE : STACEYWEBB.COM.AU
FACEBOOK: FACEBOOK.COM/STACEYWEBBEFT
INSTAGRAM: @_STACEYWEBB
LINKEDIN: LINKEDIN.COM/IN/STACEY-WEBB-0965B9238

From a young age, my heart has been deeply devoted to helping others. The urge to nurture and uplift those around me has always been an intrinsic part of who I am. It brings me immense joy to be a source of support for those in need.

When I was just 12 years old, a tragic event shook our family to its core—my father died of suicide. The pain and grief was overwhelming, but, as the eldest in a large family, I stepped forward to take on additional responsibilities.

Even though these were challenging days, I embraced these responsibilities with an open heart. Guiding and nurturing my siblings and loved ones during those difficult times only strengthened my innate desire to be a pillar of strength and support for others. This journey of compassion and care became an integral part of my identity, fuelling my determination to make a positive impact on the lives of those around me.

As I grew older, I discovered a natural gift for creating and holding nurturing spaces, allowing me to provide unwavering support to those facing the darkest moments of their lives. This realisation sparked a deep calling within me. I knew I was meant to help individuals navigate through their hardships and trauma. It was then that I firmly believed becoming a police officer would be the most meaningful and impactful way for me to serve the community.

As a police officer, I saw an opportunity to serve the community in a way that aligned with my purpose. I believe police officers hold a crucial role in being the first point of contact for someone experiencing trauma. My journey as a police officer was dedicated to being a compassionate presence and witness during moments of vulnerability. The idea of making a positive impact and truly changing people's lives felt incredibly powerful and meaningful.

With unwavering determination, I embarked on a path that led me to the police academy as soon as I could. After graduation, my journey in policing began, which meant facing demanding shift work, overtime, and mountains of paperwork. Despite the challenges, working on the frontline proved to be both fulfilling and exhilarating.

In just a few years, I found my way into the Detective offices, where my path shifted towards investigative work with greater depth. This new chapter opened doors to the intriguing world of criminal investigation, and I eagerly immersed myself in the complexities of this field. As a detective, I had the opportunity to investigate a wide range of serious crimes, but it was the sexual assault cases and coronial matters that drew me in the most. I felt a strong connection to these types of investigations, understanding the sensitivity and importance they held.

Each case I encountered brought its own set of unique challenges with individuals involved experiencing their own set of traumas.

Nonetheless, I was driven by the deep desire to provide support to those in need during their darkest moments whilst investigating. As I delved deeper into the realm of criminal investigation, I learned more about trauma, the nervous system, and how to support people with a compassionate presence during moments of vulnerability.

Sometimes taking a statement from a victim can take hours, or even days. As much as it was about collating the information and to investigate the matter thoroughly, it was also about creating and holding space for the person making the statement. Supporting and co-regulating with their nervous system, where they felt safe enough to tell you the information you needed, even amidst their experience of trauma.

When I had reached my 12-years of service in the Police Force, I had completed my family with four beautiful children—my last pregnancy being twins.

Following my maternity leave with my first child, I made a conscious decision to transition into a part-time role as a detective, opting to work one shift less than my full-time counterparts. This choice remained a constant throughout each of my pregnancies and continued in the years that followed.

I wanted to continue working as a detective after I had children. I cherished my job as a detective and the personal fulfillment it brought into my life. It was more than just a career; it was a calling to serve the community and make a meaningful impact. Having worked hard to establish myself in this role, I was not yet ready to part ways with the purpose that fuelled my passion.

However, despite being part-time on paper, my workload remained the same as that of a full-time detective. The overtime, phone calls, recall to duty, weekends, and long hours were all still there. But you know what? It didn't bother me at all! I genuinely loved my job because I felt like I was truly making a difference in people's lives. That sense of fulfillment and purpose outweighed any challenges that came with the job.

As a detective and a mother, my biggest challenge over the years has been finding that elusive balance between work and family life. My dedication to the community and the heartfelt connections with my victims and witnesses kept me fully invested in my job. A typical workday could involve a whirlwind of activities from taking statements and handling paperwork to coordinating operations and attending crime scenes and post-mortems.

Meanwhile, on the home front, my children's routines were carefully managed around my shifts, with early drop-offs at daycare and after-school care, and sometimes being the last ones to be picked up. Included in home life was supporting my kids with their homework, managing their extracurricular activities, and attending additional sessions to help my child with autism thrive. Oh, and let's not forget the daily chores of cooking, cleaning, and everything else that comes with being a parent!

The truth is, I often missed out on precious moments due to work. I couldn't always attend birthday parties or other special occasions and sometimes I was unable to take my kids to playdates or attend special school events. Thankfully, my husband, along with the support of other parents in attendance, would send me pictures and videos to keep me connected, but it still tugged at my heartstrings.

Being a perfectionist and having a fear of being seen for who I truly am led me down a path of becoming a people pleaser with almost no boundaries. I couldn't resist saying yes to every job that came my way, taking on overtime without hesitation, and accommodating late changes to shifts just to help out the office. Even when additional work was thrust upon me, I found it hard to say no because of the praise and trust I received: "Stacey, you do such a great job, and I know you'll handle this with the care it deserves."

Looking back, I'm aware that my 17 years of service in policing left me with deep emotional wounds from the traumas I encountered. After attending heartbreaking cases like child deaths or child sexual assaults, I would often come home and instinctively need to hug my children, just to reassure myself that they were safe and sound, even if they were fast asleep. Attending drownings during my service left me with lingering anxieties surrounding water and children, particularly when it involves my own kids, though this fear is slowly being released.

As a result of my experiences, I've become hyper-aware of my surroundings during conversations and often choose to sit with my back against a wall in public to keep an eye on who's moving around me. I'm also proactive in teaching my children the proper names for their body parts and educating them about body privacy and inappropriate touching from a young age.

Over the years, balancing the roles of a mother and a detective has been a constant challenge, leaving me feeling unsettled and unbalanced within myself. There were numerous occasions when I felt like I was falling short both as a mother and as a detective. These feelings were compounded by an underlying fear of never being good enough in the eyes of others. When I moved to part-time, I felt a strong need to prove myself, even though I knew deep down I was great at my job, the pressure still weighed heavily on me. When I couldn't take on overtime or handle last-minute tasks, I couldn't shake the guilt that came with it.

Of course, I deeply wanted to be there for my children celebrating their milestones, supporting their growth, helping them learn, playing with them at the park, and more. I strived to be the best mother and detective possible. But in the process, I felt I had to do it all myself, all out of the fear of not measuring up as both a mother and a detective. This constant striving for perfection left me overwhelmed, with little patience left to spare at home, and I found myself constantly stressed in every aspect of my life.

I also became conscious of the fact that I was not truly enjoying life anymore. The added work and self-imposed pressure took a toll on my self-confidence, self-esteem, and ability to set healthy boundaries. As my stress and anxiety levels soared, I unknowingly passed on this tension to my children, affecting our interactions and relationships. I would become frustrated and angry with them, though deep down, I knew they weren't the cause of my emotions.

To cope with these emotions and to avoid facing the guilt, I resorted to binge eating and drinking alcohol as a means to numb the pain. It felt like I was stuck in an unhealthy cycle of survival mode, dissociation, and auto-pilot. Beneath it all, I carried a deep anger towards myself. I was angry for not establishing my own boundaries, for failing to recognise my self-worth, and for living a life that felt incongruent with who I truly was. I felt broken.

I came to a profound realisation that change was not only necessary for my own well-being, but also for the sake of my children's future. It was this revelation that set me on a transformative path, focusing on nurturing and healing my own nervous system to break free from the clutches of the flight/fight/freeze/fawn response.

Throughout the years, I had diligently studied trauma and its impact on the nervous system, aiming to offer support and understanding to those in distress. However, I had overlooked a crucial aspect—the significance of supporting myself in the process. It was time to turn that compassion inward and prioritise my own healing journey as I sought to create a more balanced and harmonious life for myself and my children.

The beautiful journey of supporting my nervous system and embarking on a personal healing path began to unfold. I reconnected with my body, explored my sensations and emotions, became attuned to my intuition, and fostered a deep emotional release of fear and traumas with self-compassion.

At work, I started incorporating subtle somatic movements, breathwork, and Emotional Freedom Techniques (EFT or tapping) into practice, which I further explored in depth at home. As I tended to my nervous system, I granted myself the precious gift of curiosity without judgement, trusting my intuition, and allowing love to envelop my being.

Remarkably, the constant stress began to fade, and a sense

of clarity emerged within me. Instead of reacting impulsively, I learned to pause, acknowledge my emotions, and respond with greater awareness and perspective. This newfound practice deeply supported and regulated my nervous system. Empowering me to set small but meaningful boundaries, release burdens I couldn't control, and most importantly, reminded me I was never broken.

The balance between work and home—detective and mother—felt more congruent. I met and released many limiting beliefs of unworthiness that were in my path and found that my window of tolerance was wider and expansive. I was establishing meaningful boundaries without the guilt. My nervous system felt like I wasn't just surviving, but living an embodied life.

Of course, I still experienced trauma whilst being a police officer. However, instead of avoiding the emotions, pushing them aside, and hoping they would go away on its own, I made time to give those emotions attention. I used subtle somatic movements, grounding practices, breathwork, EFT, and journaling just to name a few. I learned to make myself a priority while regulating my nervous system. Sometimes this occurred during a shift, in between jobs at work, or after my shift. I would also take the time to regulate my nervous system in the car before picking up my children, before walking into the house, while the kids were busy, or whenever I could so I could show up and be present for my family. Sometimes it was a quick 2-minute session and sometimes it was longer, but, however I incorporated it, it created space within my nervous system and allowed myself to feel my feelings without judgement. I was able to give myself permission to be seen and remind myself that I am enough just as I am.

I continued my studies with trauma and the nervous system and became a Trauma-Trained Somatic Therapist certified in many other modalities including breathwork, EFT, intuition, and metaphysical sciences.

As I dove deeper into my passions, I found myself expanding into the creation of my business as an Intuitive Somatic Mentor and Coach, supporting individuals on their journey of healing and transformation. My goal is to empower their nervous system, enabling them to let go and reconnect with the innate wisdom and intelligence of their body. This process elevates their vibration and allows them to reclaim their personal power by releasing fear and trauma stored within their body.

I also found solace in writing, an art that I love deeply. It led me to publish books that aim to support others on their healing journeys and serve as a reminder that they are never alone in this vast world.

Through it all, I persevered as a mother and a detective because I deeply believed in the importance of my work and the impact it had on the community and my children. Balancing the demands of my career and my family wasn't easy, but the love and fulfillment I found in both aspects of my life made the journey worthwhile. Every step of the way, I learned to continue providing support to my nervous system, embrace the challenges, cherish the moments I could spend with my family, and make the most of every precious opportunity to create beautiful memories together.

Although I have moved away from investigating crime (that is another story), what I do now is an expansion to what I did as a detective. I am forever grateful for my first responder journey as I still continue to serve the community in a different way.

Finding a balance whilst working in any job and being a parent is a personal and individualised journey. Each parent navigates through it in their own distinctive way. Regardless of the path one takes, prioritising the support and well-being of your nervous system gives numerous benefits, no matter what challenges you face. By nurturing and caring for your nervous system, you empower yourself to meet and release limiting beliefs, fears, and traumas, enabling you to embrace the joys of parenthood while excelling in your professional endeavours.

CHERYL EDWARDES

❝ ONE OF THE THINGS THAT I FOUND WITH WORKING, AND I WOULD RECOMMEND THIS TO ALL WORKING MUMS AND DADS, IS TO BE OPEN AND HONEST WITH YOUR BOSS ABOUT WHAT IT IS THAT YOU NEED IN TERMS OF YOUR FAMILY. ❞

Cheryl is a seasoned legal professional with a diverse career spanning law, politics, and the mining industry. With over three decades of experience, she transitioned from corporate law to a prominent political career, serving in various ministerial roles including Attorney-General and Environment Minister. Recognized for her contributions, Cheryl has been honored with awards such as the Order of Australia and inclusion in the 100 Women of Influence. Currently, she brings her expertise to HHG Legal Group, where she focuses on pro bono work and spearheads the development of the firm's charitable initiatives.

CHERYL EDWARDES

AUTHOR NAME: CHERYL EDWARDES
ROLE: HONORARY SPECIAL COUNCIL AND CHAIR
ORGANISATION: HGG LEGAL
LINKEDIN: LINKEDIN.COM/IN/HON-CHERYL-EDWARDES-AM-GAICD-4A019751

SARAH:
So, can you just start by telling me a little bit about how you were raised, your childhood, and how that shaped you as a parent?

CHERYL:
I had a fabulous childhood. I'm the eldest of three girls. My mother and grandma were the strongest role models, and both of them always worked. They weren't stay-at-home mums whatsoever. Their motto in life was, "There is nothing you cannot do if you set your mind to it." And so, I've always lived by that. I mean, they just provided a really good upbringing. They were very supportive in whatever you wanted to do. If you wanted to become a vegetarian, no problem. If you wanted to go back to just introducing fish, no worries. You wanted to go back to meat, no problems. I mean, you know, I think back... How difficult that might have been! They would drop you everywhere, pick you up whenever you needed it. You know, whatever you needed or wanted to do, they were there to support your decision-making.

SARAH:

That is so great. And in terms of your career, what did you start doing before you had children?

CHERYL:

I left school at 15, got a job at Woolworths just around the corner from where I lived as a checkout operator. I did that for the whole of those school holidays and never went back to school. I was then transferred from the checkout into the office. The manager of the store was amazing in teaching how you could run an office. One of the things I remember very clearly was having a clean desk. So, if you left your desk clean at night-time, when you walked in in the morning, your desk was clean, and you knew exactly where to start. To get everything done through a day, it taught me a lot in terms of setting out what your job was, to what you had to do in a day, in a week, in a month. It was such good training even up until now; I remember very clearly those rules. I just continued to do different jobs from there and went back to uni. I had some fabulous jobs. I mean, I worked in the library at UWA. I worked in the museum as their records clerk. I had the opportunity of going and getting records off our professor's desks and actually categorising them, which was fabulous. I then spent a number of years working at a firm of chartered accountants, doing all of the calculations and reporting. One of the things that I found with working, and I would recommend this to all working mums and dads, is to be open and honest with your boss about what it is that you need in terms of your family. And I said when I had my firstborn, I wanted to be at home but I also wanted to work, and so, I worked three days a week. This is back in the days before you had computers, so they sent the work out by taxi, dropped it off, I did the work, rang up a taxi, sent it back… It really goes to show how if you wanna get it done, you can get it done!

I always took the day off for school sports day, and it was amazing. By the time mobile phones were in vogue, Scotty, my second born, would tell me what he needed for me to bring for lunch, not just for him, but for all of his mates.

SARAH:
Oh, that's brilliant. And you had your sons quite far apart, didn't you?

CHERYL:
15 years apart, yes.

SARAH:
And did you notice a big difference in terms of the ability to work while you had a baby? I just love the fact that you were able to do that in that generation because it's quite rare to hear that happened. How do you think that came about in terms of you as a person? Do you think it was really the fact that you communicated so well, and you were lucky in terms of the company, or how do you think that came about?

CHERYL:
I think it's always been that I've always asked, and in all of my jobs and roles, I was never refused. And I think if you put forward an argument as to the value of it, all companies that I've worked with have accepted that value. And it was always, for instance, a night-time routine; get home for the meals, the bed, the bedtime story, etc. And then, if need be, go back to work. And sometimes that meant driving back into the office, you know, until the time when Zoom came around and you can do your work like that. When my firstborn was wanting to go to childcare, we didn't have childcare for under two-year-olds, so you made other arrangements.

SARAH:
It's really interesting. I love the fact that you did it! And how long

did you do that for? How old was your son when you when you went back to doing that?

CHERYL:

First one—three months. Second one, I didn't stop. I mean, I had the highest telephone bill that any patient has ever had at Glengarry Hospital because I kept working while I was in the hospital!

SARAH:

So in between, the difference between your firstborn and your second born, would it really be just the difference in terms of the ability to work from home and the, I guess the accessibility of having a phone and things like that, that would have been the biggest difference for you?

CHERYL:

Not quite because when the second was born that was still 1986, so access to computers and mobile phones still wasn't available. I think I got my first mobile phone in 1989, and it was a brick! I mean, you can't believe how big and heavy and bulky they were.

SARAH:

Yeah, and your work has obviously progressed as the times gone on and you've worked in quite male-dominated industries. How have you found that as a mum?

CHERYL:

I have never had any trouble. I never experienced harassment. I never experienced any discrimination until I got to politics, but you know, it's politics—it's always about the politics more than any of it being personal. But no, that is not to say I haven't observed it. I have, and I've always gone in to help a female colleague. And that's one of the things that I would encourage all women to do, to help your colleagues because it's essentially for you, too. To get promoted, it's important to have female team members around you, not just to do it on your own.

SARAH:
Absolutely, and I guess with regards to your background, which I think has really set you up in terms of your personality and your confidence to have those conversations. Do you think that's what really allowed you to have that confidence within a male-dominated industry as well? And that's why you probably didn't have many problems?

CHERYL:
Yeah, look, I'm sure that's the case, and every single one of us is different, so it's about each one of us working out how you can do it for yourself and not always relying on others. You actually have to chart your own course and know yourself where you want to go. I know that there are working mums who don't want to be working. They want to be at home. I know that working mums who feel guilty about working and feel guilty about liking their job.

SARAH:
And what support did you have in terms of external support?

CHERYL:
I had a list of 13 babysitters for baby number two. And of course, as he got older, he didn't want to come to events—I was involved in politics by that time—and he didn't want to always come with us to whatever function it was. And he would work out who on the list of 13 babysitters he wanted. So, it was him who was choosing who was going to babysit, not us.

SARAH:
That's brilliant. And was your husband supportive throughout

your career in terms of his fair share? What did he do for work while you were a public servant?

CHERYL:

So, both federal and state, and very supportive. I couldn't have done it without his support. Every Sunday we would work out what we were doing in terms of our diaries, who was going to be home, who wasn't, who was doing the meal. I used to time it so that Colin got home before me. There was one occasion, with the firstborn, when Colin and I were all walking out the door, about to lock up the door, and we looked back, and we saw the second born sitting in his bouncer, and we're thinking, "Oh, this didn't work... we forgot to talk here."

SARAH:

That's really lovely that you had his support. And again, was that quite an open communication thing that you had with him? Did he have a similar upbringing to you, or was it an education piece for him?

CHERYL:

Yeah, actually, I think you're right. His mum always worked. In fact, she worked right up until she passed in her 80s. Yeah, I think that makes a very big difference to how men view their part in parenthood. It's how they've obviously been raised as well, which is very interesting.

It's interesting, the reflections too, because both of us, my husband and I, did our studies part-time to get our degrees. And our kids thought that was normal. They thought that's how you do it. You work and study part-time. Until we told them, "Oh no, you can go full-time!"

SARAH:

What in terms of challenges would you say were the biggest ones when you were trying to juggle being a working mum?

CHERYL:

It's interesting looking back now. You can't remember the challenges, but they were there. When the second born was really ill and in ICU, I took the night shift, Colin took leave so he could take the day shift, you know, all of those things. You just do it.

SARAH:

If you were to give a key bit of advice to a working mum, what would that be?

CHERYL:

Ask for help, you know, you can't do it on your own. And you're not expected to do it on your own. Ask for help. It doesn't hurt. It doesn't matter. It's not saying anything about your inability to be able to be a working mum. It's very normal.

SARAH:

And just from your perspective as an employee, do you have employees that sit under you now?

CHERYL:

No, but I always made sure that throughout my career when I had employees, and particularly in my legal offices, to let the young lawyers know they didn't have to stay there until eight o'clock at night to prove themselves. Go home, be there for dinner, do the bath, do the bedtime story, and then come back to work that evening if needed.

Another thing that I did was to always bring the kids into the office so that they knew where I work, what I did. And when I worked weekends, I would also make sure there was always something they could do, like, "Look after the paper clips, the bulldog clips," or whatever it was. It's very important that they know where you are. I always made sure that they could always ring me at any time, day or night. Often it was, you know, they wanted to know if they could have the leftovers in the fridge. And of course, given the fact that I'd been away for three or four days, right, I didn't know what leftovers were in the fridge. So, I couldn't help but tell them to smell and see. You know, "Has it got green stuff on it?" So bringing kids into the office is something I would let my employees do, you know, within reason.

SARAH:
Haha, I love it. And so did you work away quite a bit as well?

CHERYL:
Yeah, I did a lot of travel, particularly when I was a minister, and, you know, if ever I could do it, I would travel over school holidays so I could take one of them with me.

The hotels are amazing nowadays, and even back then, I mean, I'm talking, you know, 20, 30 years ago. They would welcome young Scott with presents, toys, whatever. One of the workers would come up in the morning and take him for a walk while I finished getting dressed. And then, they actually organised a babysitter for me for the three, four days I was there. And then they would do what he wanted—he got to see more of the place than I did! He had a fabulous time. And that's the thing, I think it's looking at it from a different perspective sometimes and making the most out of situations rather than thinking that I've got to travel and be away from them.

I mean, there were other times when I was a practicing lawyer, and I would come home and find him on the phone, talking to one of my legal clients. So what? He was creating the confidence that he had in terms of being able to talk to anybody. Richard Court, when he was the Premier of Western Australia, would often ring to talk to me, Scott would answer the phone and they would be having a great conversation before I actually got on the phone. But, again, that's instilling some confidence in him.

I was just interviewing a young woman before we got on the Zoom for a role, and she had her eight-month-old sitting on her lap, and I remember I did that with our second child as well, regularly. So yeah, sitting on the lap whilst I was on the phone or on the computer.

You know, it's life, it's bringing them up, not separating them out from your life. You're making them part of your life. And I think that's really important to have the confidence to do that and not feel that it has to be one or the other. It's all intertwined—your personal and your professional life. And I think that's a really important message to deliver to other people as well. I think some women feel like it has to be really segregated, and they don't have the confidence to do things like that. Nobody else really cares at the end of the day, as long as you can do what you do.

Some roles, though, are different. If you're a teacher, obviously that's a different role. If you're a nurse, you know, also a different role. So, it depends on the role, but do what you can and what you need to do in your role and try to involve your children as much as you can.

TANIA GOMEZ

> BY ACTIVELY ENGAGING IN WORK, I FEEL A SENSE OF PURPOSE AND FULFILLMENT THAT POSITIVELY IMPACTS BOTH MY PERSONAL AND PROFESSIONAL LIFE.

Tania Gomez is a dynamic entrepreneur passionate about helping NDIS (National Disability Insurance Scheme) providers thrive. With over a decade of business ownership experience, Tania has founded four successful ventures: Provider+, Strawberry Solutions, Tania Gomez Consulting, and Jelli Beanz. Her mission is to assist providers in overcoming challenges and achieving business success. Tania's expertise, energy, and dedication to quality and compliance drive her commitment to helping providers reach their goals. As an NDIS Auditor since 2019, Tania brings extensive experience to her consulting work. With qualifications including a Master of Education (Leadership), Graduate Certificate of Disability Practice Management, and Bachelor of Education (Early Childhood), and Currently completing a Doctorate of Philosophy (PHD), she is well-equipped to make a difference. Tania's ultimate passion lies in helping purpose-led businesses prioritise quality and sustainability, delivering exceptional outcomes for their clients.

TANIA GOMEZ

AUTHOR NAME: TANIA GOMEZ
BUSINESS NAME: STRAWBERRY SOLUTIONS & TANIA GOMEZ CONSULTING
POSITION: MANAGING DIRECTOR
BUSINESS INDUSTRY: EDUCATION AND BUSINESS ADVISORY
WEBSITE: WWW.STRAWBERRYSOLUTIONS.COM.AU & WWW.TANIAGOMEZ.COM.AU
INSTAGRAM: @TANIAGOMEZCONSULTING

I grew up in Sydney's inner west as an only child to a single mother. My mum, a Registered Nurse, worked tirelessly at local nursing homes and hospitals, often on shift rotations. Financially, things were tight due to her single income which taught me the value of hard work from an early age. I found agency and independence in earning my own money and started working at a young age. At eight years old, I launched my first business called 'Roll over Rover' where my neighbourhood friends and I walked and cared for local dogs during school holidays.

From that point on, I sought various ways to earn extra money so I could buy candies from the corner shop, or as I grew older, purchasing cosmetics from the chemist. Between the ages of 12 and 17 I had a string of jobs, including assisting at local markets and managing a mail order business on my street where I took orders and delivered them to the post office. I also worked at several fast-food chains such as McDonalds, Burger King, Starbucks, and Gloria Jeans.

When I moved out of home at 17, I had to support myself financially, covering expenses like food and rent. Since then, I've mostly worked full-time with the exception of a few maternity leave periods. For me, work has always been an opportunity to acquire new skills, exercise autonomy, earn money, and give me a sense of escapism.

Reflecting on my childhood, I realised that resilience and an unwavering drive for independence was instilled in me at a young age. Work provided a sense of control over my future when other aspects of life were uncertain.

While I can appreciate the resilience and determination I developed, I also experienced loneliness and isolation at times. And as I considered raising my own children, I aspired to take a different approach. I had to learn to ask for help and rely on support from others, whether it be from my husband, friends, or even my staff. I knew I wanted to provide my children with a sense of support, security, and certainty about their futures. I wanted them to feel confident in seeking assistance when faced with challenges.

My journey as a working mother began when I embarked on a career as a childcare worker and later became an Early Childhood Teacher. Initially, I had a deep desire to be a mother and envisioned spending my days with my little ones. After the birth of my first son, Charlie, I had planned to take 12 months of maternity leave from my role teaching students in their Diploma of Early Childhood. However, after six months of leave, I found myself longing to return to work.

Although I cherished the time spent with Charlie, I often felt overwhelmed by the demands of caring for a baby, and I yearned for more mental stimulation. While this need for stimulation made me feel guilty, I realised that my personal fulfillment in pursuing my professional goals and utilising my expertise would allow me to make more meaningful contributions, not only to my family, but also to my community, and my sector.

Financial independence was another significant factor of why I wanted to return to the workforce. Growing up in a single income home, I wanted to ensure my family was well taken care of and provided for. And as the daughter of a self-sufficient mother, I didn't want to rely on my husband to be the sole provider in our home. Being a working mother allowed me to contribute to our household financially, ensuring a level of security and the ability to make financial choices for my family's well-being. I also wanted my presence as a "working mum" to serve as a positive role model for my children. I wanted to demonstrate the importance of pursuing one's passions and finding a sense of purpose outside of parenting.

My work provides me with a sense of personal growth, intellectual stimulation, and social interaction, contributing to my overall well-being and happiness, which, for me, is super important to teach my kids.

Being a working mother has allowed me to strike a balance between nurturing my family and pursuing my own professional aspirations. It has empowered me to lead a fulfilling life, while also inspiring my children to dream big and break down gender stereotypes. Having three boys and a little girl, I feel even more passionate about being a good role model today than when I was a new mum.

I have faced numerous challenges being a working mum, but perhaps the biggest one was the weight of expectations I placed upon myself. I felt the need to excel in every aspect of my life; to be the best mother, wife, and boss. At times, this drive was motivating and inspiring, but it also became a heavy burden to carry. Instead of asking for help, I often tried to do it all on my own. Perhaps it was the years of independence that made seeking assistance difficult, and I didn't want my children or family to miss out. This often resulted in me stretching myself thin as I pursued studies, work, and being a business owner—something I'll get to shortly!

There are moments where I feel like I am failing in some way. Simple things, like forgetting to book time off work to attend a school assembly or remembering the last-minute craft item my child needed for school, can throw me off balance. While the lapses may seem small, they magnify the pressure I put on myself and make me question my ability to juggle all my responsibilities effectively.

I have also encountered workplace barriers as a working mother. The glass ceiling was a real obstacle, being overlooked for promotions due to assumptions made by male bosses about my future plans of having more children. Overcoming this hurdle required a significant shift in my approach. It led me to make the decision to become self-employed, which not only increased my salary but also provided me with a greater degree of flexibility and control.

Becoming self-employed had a transformative effect on my career trajectory. It allowed me to have more autonomy over my professional growth and strike a better work/life balance. By taking this step, I gained increased financial stability and the freedom to shape my own schedule, ensuring I could be present for both my family and my work commitments. It also allows me to hire other working mothers and provide them with a safe, flexible, and rewarding work environment.

Fast forward to today with four children and four businesses in tow, and I still struggle with the balance of it all. But while the days often seem too short, they are filled with goals I'm chasing, dreams I'm achieving, and a house full of love and laughter.

I firmly believe that our own happiness is our responsibility. For me, finding a meaningful form of work and making contributions to my family and community are essential components of my happiness. By actively engaging in work, I feel a sense of purpose and fulfillment that positively impacts both my personal and professional life.

To balance being a working mother, I have developed a highly organised approach. I prioritise scheduling my workdays around my children's commitments, aiming to align my hours with their school schedule as closely as possible. Living in WA while having clients in NSW or QLD has proven beneficial for balance due to the time difference. Early mornings are a trade-off, but it means my phone and emails generally slow down by 3:00pm each day, granting me the entire afternoon to spend with my children. In that approach there is balance—hectic mornings and calm afternoons.

Though I strive for excellent organisation, there are times when unforeseen circumstances disrupt my plans which can result in additional work hours. However, with the support of my husband, we navigate these situations knowing they are temporary and find ways to manage them effectively.

I also try to book at least one week off work during the school holidays. This dedicated break allows me to focus on being present with my children, gives me time to mentally recharge, and provides space to think more strategically about work. It also provides an opportunity to delegate tasks within the business, helping to alleviate some of my workload. Thinking about how I can do things smarter, rather than harder is something I have consistently worked at.

By combining effective scheduling, leveraging the time difference, and creating dedicated breaks, I have found a balance that allows me to fulfill both my professional and parental responsibilities. It's an ongoing process that requires adaptability, but with careful planning and the support of my family, I have for the most part, been able to create a harmonious integration of work and family life.

The greatest support I have received is from my husband, who has been an incredible partner in sharing the responsibilities of parenting, household tasks, and work commitments. Currently, we both work together in our own business, allowing us to effectively balance work and home responsibilities. However, it hasn't always been this way. Up until three years ago, my husband had a demanding corporate job, which limited our flexibility and made juggling our responsibilities more challenging.

During a particularly difficult period, my husband had a lengthy commute to work of two hours each way, every day. That's four hours just commuting! At the time, we lived away from our families, so I was left with three young children at home without any external support. We sought assistance with live-in au pairs, which proved to be a valuable form of support, especially in managing childcare duties. Those were challenging times, and as they say, the days felt long, but the years passed quickly.

We knew we had to reassess our situation and find a better way forward. So, we decided that it was time for my husband to start his own business! This decision was pivotal in providing us with the support and flexibility we needed to navigate the demands of work and parenting more effectively. While we initially faced difficulties, we were able to find a solution that worked for our family's needs. Being able to reflect on our life and make necessary adjustments allowed us to find a better balance, ensuring that we can fulfill our responsibilities as parents while pursuing our professional goals.

As I previously mentioned, I was 17 when I embarked on my career in Early Childhood and later transitioned into leadership roles within Vocational Education and Training. While I enjoyed these positions, the demanding nature of the job, including long days, travel, and the associated pressure, posed challenges when I was trying to conceive my third child. Recognising the need for a change, I made the decision to resign and leverage my educational skills to establish an eLearning agency called Strawberry Solutions in 2016. This marked my second entrepreneurial venture, which has since grown to employ over 40 staff and collaborate with renowned global brands such as Breville, Johnson & Johnson, the Housing Industry Association, and Fire and Rescue NSW. Through this business, I get to utilise my educational expertise, indulge in my passion for technology, and experience the creative fulfillment that it offers.

Additionally, I founded a NDIS consultancy called Provider+, which, since 2019, has registered over 5,000 NDIS providers, capturing a significant market share of 53%. In March 2023, I made the decision to sell this business. Currently, I run Tania Gomez Consulting, where I assist NDIS providers in surpassing compliance requirements and developing quality systems and processes to facilitate their growth and scalability.

Throughout my journey, I have always been drawn to business growth and the process of building something from the ground up. However, the choice to step away from the safety of my corporate role and venture into the unknown was largely driven by my vision of aligning my work with my family life and creating a better day-to-day balance for us.

I believe I have a growth mindset and I am an eternal optimist. I approach every situation with a willingness to learn and grow, seeking valuable lessons and finding the silver lining in almost anything. My passion and commitment extend to both my family and the pursuit of a fulfilling life. I strive to create a legacy that my children can proudly share with future generations.

My best advice to any new mother would be to trust your own instincts and not base decisions on other people's opinions or expectations. It's important to follow your own path and prioritise your own happiness. Too often, we worry about how others will perceive our choices, whether it's deciding to work or stay at home. We may feel pressured to conform to family traditions, the opinions of friends, or societal norms, without truly considering what is best for ourselves and our families.

Listen to that inner voice or intuition that guides you. Tune into what feels right and brings you joy. We should not underestimate the power of our own judgment in making decisions that align with our needs and values. It's essential to trust ourselves more and not give away our power to societal demands or external judgments.

Recognise that what feels right today may change tomorrow, and that is perfectly okay. Embrace adaptability and understand that our needs and circumstances evolve. Be open to reassessing and adjusting your decisions as you navigate the journey of motherhood and work.

Finding a balance between being a new mother and pursuing your own fulfillment can be both challenging and rewarding. Embrace the journey with all its complexities, knowing that it's okay to face difficulties along the way. Embracing your own happiness and following your bliss will ultimately lead you to a fulfilling and authentic life.

SARAH COLEMAN

❝ LET'S SHARE MORE OF THE HARD STUFF, LET'S NORMALISE THE NOT-SO-GREAT DAYS, AND LET'S ALL BE AMAZING ADVOCATES FOR EACH OTHER AND THE MUCH-NEEDED DIVERSITY OF THOUGHT WE EACH BRING TO THE WORKPLACE WHEN WE SHOW UP AS OUR TRUE, AUTHENTIC, MESSY, AND UNIQUE SELVES ❞

Sarah, a proud mum of three, is the CEO of idoba, a digital transformation company dedicated to solving mining's toughest challenges. She is passionate about creating a better future for the mining sector and beyond by co-creating solutions that leverage human and artificial intelligence, as well as leading-edge technology and innovation. She founded and grew two successful companies, ImpRes and Sandpit Innovation, that specialised in business improvement and technology development for the resources industry; both are now part of idoba. Sarah has been recognised for her excellence and leadership by several awards and honours, including Women in Industry Excellence in Mining, WA Business News 40 Under 40, AIM WA State Owner-Manager of the Year, and CME Most Outstanding Young Female Finalist.

SARAH COLEMAN

AUTHOR NAME: SARAH COLEMAN
BUSINESS NAME: IDOBA
POSITION: CEO
BUSINESS INDUSTRY: MINING
WEBSITE: WWW.IDOBA.COM
SOCIAL MEDIA: HTTPS://WWW.LINKEDIN.COM/IN/SARAH-COLEMAN-6439415/

I am a proud mum of three: my stepdaughter Lily, my son Ollie, and my daughter Maisie. I am also incredibly privileged to have an amazing husband, Shane, who, after a 20+ year career in mining, stepped out to take on the role as the primary caregiver. I know how lucky I am to be in this situation, so I don't want to create any illusion that I do what I do without the amazing support I have from Shane. While I work, he ensures the kids get to school, makes their lunches, handles the cleaning, washing, and cooking, and ensures that when I get home, I can just be there for the kids. I know he doesn't have it easy either. I often say that while we have a long way to go in many industries to see females in senior leadership roles, I believe we have even further to go in accepting fathers being the primary caregiver.

Even with the support I have from Shane, like many working mums, I struggle with the battle of the heart to just show up at work each day. I love what I do, but some days are really hard.

There was one particular day when I had to deliver a speech to an audience of over 1,300 people (no pressure!), and that morning my daughter was feeling unwell and came to seek comfort from me. It was 2:00am, but all she wanted was her mum. My mind was racing with thoughts of needing to sleep, the upcoming presentation, and the necessity to appear alert and knowledgeable. I looked at my five-year-old daughter, and seeing the distress in her eyes, my heart took over. In that moment, I realised that my most important role was simply to be there for her.

Later that day, as I was waiting to go on stage—and feeling so exhausted—I started reflecting on the horrendous winter of sickness myself and every other working mum I know had that year (the first year "post-COVID"). While my speech already included a traditional Acknowledgment of Country, I pulled out my pen and quickly wrote a unique recognition, dedicated to working mums. Upon taking the stage, I shared my 2:00am experience and extended a special acknowledgment to all the working mums in the audience who grapple with similar heartfelt struggles every day. That acknowledgment got a massive round of applause before I'd even started my speech.

It really made me stop and think... Why do we not share more of this? Why is there such emphasis on the importance of vulnerability in the workplace, yet there's a persistent pressure to maintain an image of perfection, as if we have everything under control? The notion of being a "supermum" who flawlessly juggles work and family life is not only unrealistic but also sets a daunting standard, making other working mothers feel inadequate because they are struggling to get out the door each day with their shoes on! What stops us from being able to share our authentic selves? That messy, imperfect, unique, and authentic person we often feel like we have to hide behind a smattering of lipstick (if we remember) and maybe a suit (if we get time to iron it!)?

While that moment of presenting was only about 18 months ago, I've inadvertently made it my mission each time I do a speech to share more stories like that one to help start normalising some of the sharing. Moments like my children tearfully pleading, "Mummy, don't go again," as I head off to work, or their questions of, "Why can't you be like other mums and take us to school?" Alongside these are the daily mishaps that life throws our way: broken bones, sick pets, my husband needing an Uber to the hospital because I was unreachable in meetings, or even household incidents like ceilings caving in. These are the sorts of challenges (big and small) mothers balance while managing our daily work responsibilities.

The truth is, I didn't start out being a massive advocate for females and mums in the workplace. In fact, when I started my career in mining after graduating from a double degree in Mechanical Engineering and Commerce, I used to think that because I'd chosen a male-dominated industry, I couldn't expect to get treated differently. My first role out of university was working in an aluminium smelter in Tasmania. I was not a very good mechanical engineer; I lasted about six months, but I quickly moved into more people leadership and improvement roles—which I loved. It taught me a lot about what motivates people and how you can get the best out of them. My career with Rio Tinto saw me move from Tasmania to Western Australia where I again held various leadership roles. At the age of 28, I was made the leader of the business improvement function for all the Rio Tinto Iron Ore operations. I was the youngest in the team and one of very few female leaders in the business at that time. Talk about an induction of fire. I had one new team member say, "I refuse to work for someone who is old enough to be my daughter," …which made for some interesting one-on-one coaching discussions!

In early 2010, I left Rio Tinto and took a massive leap of faith by founding and running my own businesses. I started a company called Improvement Resources, an operational improvement consultancy, and a few years later, joined forces with a colleague to start a second company, Sandpit Innovation, a technology and innovation business. During that time, I had two disastrous personal relationships, both of which cost me significantly—financially and psychologically—and I had to basically rebuild myself and my finances both times. A few years in, the iron ore market crashed and I had to make 37 people redundant in one day (which was tough when there were only 52 people in the business). I have been unfairly accused of many things that impacted the businesses, and in the early days, I had many people attempt to take advantage of me and my successes because I was a young female in business (after all, what would I know!). I was diagnosed with endometriosis two years into starting the businesses, which is incredibly painful. Following many laparoscopies and thankfully after being able to naturally conceive my babies, I had a hysterectomy at the age of 39. Talk about a lesson in resilience and self-belief, which is never easy when the inner critic in your head is so strong.

With all the lows, there were some amazing highs. I was a WA Business News 40 Under 40 recipient, named the AIM WA State Owner/Manager of the year, was a finalist in the CME Most Outstanding Young Female in Mining, and most recently, I was named the winner of the 2022 'Women In Industry' Excellence in Mining Award. At the peak, the combined businesses generated nearly $20M of revenue, and in one year alone, we employed over 100 people to work on various projects. Of course, the biggest high was meeting Shane, becoming a bonus mum to my stepdaughter, and having my son and daughter. I have travelled to some incredible places and worked with some of the most inspiring leaders in the mining sector. In 2020 I sold both businesses to Perenti, and as part of that sale, I became the CEO of a new venture called idoba. idoba is on a mission to reshape mining with cutting-edge software products, our DiiMOS™ platform, and expert consulting. As the CEO of idoba, I am also a member of the Group Executive Committee of Perenti, a mining services company with 11,000 employees globally.

What have I learned from all that? Obviously, apart from the times I think I am completely crazy for what I have taken on, there are many lessons learned—the best ones coming from my mistakes. There is the importance of resilience, grit, courage, backing yourself, and never taking no for an answer (even when you are scared, and you don't think you are good enough). There is the power of vulnerability and how, in a moment by sharing a bit of yourself, you give other people the opportunity to share a bit of themselves... unravelling the perception of "normal" one interaction at a time. Then there is curiosity, the drive to constantly ask questions, to seek understanding, and to challenge the status quo. This curiosity has not only helped me to grow personally but has also fostered a culture of continuous sharing, unmasking, and helping people show up as their authentic selves. It's about being willing to learn, to admit when you don't know something, and to be open to new ideas and perspectives, without the fear of being judged. This approach has led to more collaborative and dynamic team environments, where everyone feels valued and empowered to contribute.

If I go back to one of my early comments, I didn't start out being a massive advocate for women and mothers in the industry. This has changed a lot for me over time. I often recall two amazing ladies who worked in my team at Rio Tinto when I was leading business improvement at 28. They were both working part-time as they had young children. When I look back, I wonder if I was supportive enough of them? Of course, as the cliché goes, it often takes becoming a mum to realise just how hard it is and how important it is to normalise some of the challenges. If I'm very honest with myself, I did not support them the way they needed to be supported. I expected them to just show up like everyone else; I expected them to be as available and as committed as their full-time counterparts, not fully appreciating the juggling act they were performing. Looking back, I realise I could have done more to accommodate their unique situations and to acknowledge the extraordinary effort they were making to balance their professional and personal responsibilities. This realisation has since shaped my approach to leadership. I now strive to create a more inclusive and understanding work environment, where the needs and challenges of all team members, especially working parents, are recognised and supported. The key for me is how do we build organisations that work for people, not just having people work for an organisation.

When I am having hard days, I reflect on a quote my daughter said to me when she was five. She was playing with a toy plane and turned to me and said, "Mummy, when I grow up, I want to be a fighter pilot." Then she paused, turned around, and looked carefully at me and said, "Actually no, when I grow up, I want to be a normal mummy and go to work." It was in that moment that I knew I, and other working mothers (like my own amazing mum who set the standard for me), were making a difference. We are rewriting what "normal" looks like for the next generation. So, here's to all the "normal mummy's" doing what we do each day just to show up. Let's share more of the hard stuff, let's normalise the not-so-great days, and let's all be amazing advocates for each other and the much-needed diversity of thought we each bring to the workplace when we show up as our true, authentic, messy, and unique selves.

KERRY McNAMEE

> DURING TIMES WHEN I WASN'T WORKING, I FELT LOST, UNINSPIRED, LONELY (WHILE NEVER ACTUALLY BEING ALONE), FLAT, AND JUST A BIT EMPTY.

Kerry McNamee, a British woman who migrated to Perth, Australia, is a mother of two children: Callum, who is five, and Amelia, who is four. Both kids possess unique personalities, keeping Kerry on her toes each day! She learns a lot from her children and cherishes the life they are building together in Perth as a family. In her professional life, Kerry works in Human Resources for a large construction company, and she is pleased to say that she genuinely enjoys her work. Kerry and her family relish spending time outdoors, engaging in arts and crafts, and taking delight in solving puzzles together.

KERRY McNAMEE

AUTHOR NAME: KERRY McNAMEE
POSITION: HUMAN RESOURCES
BUSINESS INDUSTRY: CONSTRUCTION
LINKEDIN: LINKEDIN.COM/IN/KERRY-MC-NAMEE-A90B7B133

When I'm asked what my childhood was like, I have to admit it brings about an overall feeling of discomfort. For me, it's not easy to explain. By no means was it awful and nor did I suffer any of the heartbreaking traumas some others have. But that doesn't mean to say it was easy or free from adversity.

My parents divorced when I was around five. My mum said she left the house with just us—my two sisters and me—and a few bags of clothes. I have very few memories of my dad being around, but similarly, I don't have many of my mum either. According to her, she worked multiple jobs while studying at university with the aim of providing a better life for us. I grew up in complete awe of her. I felt incredibly inspired by her resilience and determination to overcome the multitude of challenges thrown her way. I remember writing mini essays in all her special occasion cards, trying to put into words how grateful I was to have her as my mum, and how I wanted to be as devoted to my children as she was to us.

Fast forward 34 years, and my mum is no longer in my life. It was January 17, 2021; I called her mobile just as I did nearly every single day. Instead of the usual ringtone, it was an automated message: "The number you have called is no longer in service."

After frantic calls to my sisters and messages to my mum's partner, we learned that she chose to cut all ties with my sisters and me, and there was the expectation that we should respect her decision given everything she had done for us over the years. Confused? Yep, me too. Now, it would be pertinent to mention that mental health challenges were prominent in our household, and I am fully versed in the devastating impact this can have. And perhaps ultimately, her mental health issues grew bigger than her desire to have her family around. But we won't ever really know.

A lot of questions have been raised throughout the process of us trying to understand and accept Mum's decision. Most of these remain unanswered, and I'm left wondering what parts of my childhood were real, what was fabricated, and what parts were simply muddled in a web of lies and exaggerated truths. I have so many questions, questions that I will never be able to uncover the truth to. And there is nothing I can do about it. What I can do, however, is vow to never lie to my own children, never to make them question anything I tell them, and to make them feel secure, loved, wanted, treasured, and wholeheartedly accepted. Now, forever, and always. Which is a nice segue into why I am a working mum.

Being a working mum was not something I actively chose to do; it wasn't a conscious decision I made. At the risk of sounding cliché, I just enjoy working. I love the work I do and have worked hard over the years to get to where I am. As a naturally driven person, I have applied myself to everything I do—even sometimes to my detriment. I am conscious of my need to achieve and be recognised for my achievements, but regardless of this, I take pride in the person I have become.

Reflecting on my childhood and how this shaped my thoughts on being a working parent, there are a few ways I look at this. Firstly, I always wanted financial independence. It's important for me not to need to rely on anyone else or to be consumed by debt. Secondly, I am proud of where I am today, of the experiences I have had, the places I have travelled to, and the future I am building for my children—most of which wouldn't be possible without working. I want my children to understand the importance of owning their own path, being responsible for their own future, and understanding financial security. In no way does this mean that I place an emphasis on wealth; it's more about the value of money and where it comes from. Finally, I hope to inspire my children, motivate them to enjoy what they do, seek balance in life, appreciate the importance of being true to themselves, and look after their well-being.

It's true what they say: being a mum is a privilege. It's the most rewarding and, equally, the most challenging thing I have ever done. Every day there are challenges, some new and some the same as the day before. There is no magic formula. You can be as organised as you can, but sometimes it's just bloody hard! Throw working full-time into the mix, along with living 9,000 miles from extended family, and it becomes a whole new meaning to 'fun and games.'

My path to motherhood wasn't easy. My brilliant son, now five, was conceived via IVF, and my daughter, age four, was our beautiful surprise baby who was conceived when my son was less than five months old. The reason I share this is because it feeds into what I believe is the biggest challenge as a working mum, something that I am still working to overcome. This would be the constant battle of feeling guilty. I absolutely adore my children, they are my world, my reason, my why, and the loves of my life. Everything I do, I do for them, and myself, either directly or indirectly. I know it sounds cliché, but it's true. As a full-time working mum, I have a constant—pretty much daily—battle of feeling guilty, especially as my journey to motherhood was tough. I don't go to work to be away from my kids, although some days it can be a nice break from the tantrums, I go to work because I enjoy what I do. I feel guilty because I know it's time away from my children. Not only do I get "mum-guilt", but I get "work-guilt" too.

On a day-to-day basis, this is what I feel guilty for:
- Being at work instead of being at home.
- Being at home instead of working extra hours.
- Rushing the kids out the door in the mornings so I can get to work.
- Not getting to work early, or even just at the same time as my colleagues.
- Getting annoyed at the kids for not being able to understand my request for them to get their shoes and socks on (even after asking nicely 20 times).
- Not being able to spend more time helping my son with his reading or writing.
- Not being able to play Monopoly or Uno at 8:00am, even when my son asks in the most polite, sweet, and loving way ever (cue the pulling heartstrings and violin music).
- Not being able to get my work done a day before the scheduled due date.
- Cutting my daughter's rendition of 'Let It Go' short because we need to get in the car to go to daycare (even if I have heard it—and joined in—50 times already that morning).
- For getting frustrated because the kids won't go to sleep on time so I can have just 30 minutes to myself before I fall into bed exhausted.
- For not being the best version of myself, for not taking care of myself like I need to, for not prioritising myself as well as the kids.
- For prioritising myself and going for a walk when I could be at home playing games with the kids.

Some days it feels as though I just can't win. But when I think about it, who am I trying to win against? Myself? Yep, that's it. So, when I find my thoughts escalating about how guilty I feel for doing or not doing something, I remind myself that no one else is putting the pressure on me other than myself. I am in control of my thoughts, my feelings, and my actions. It's impossible to do everything and be everything to everyone, and that's totally okay! I ask my children to do their best and be their best, and as a good friend of mine says, your best is good enough. I have had to let go of unrealistically high expectations I hold for myself. I remind myself regularly that it's okay if I haven't vacuumed this week or if the kids had porridge for dinner. They are fed, clothed, happy, healthy, and loved. No one is judging me, and if they are, they aren't 'my people'.

While this is easier said than done, my mind is more at ease when I am prepared for the day or week ahead. I am naturally a very organised individual and there's a lot to be said for solid preparation and coordination to make being a working mum more manageable. Most dinners are cooked at the weekend for the next day or two, with other batches popped in the freezer. Washing is done on weekends with clothes dried, folded, and put away. And preparing the kid's uniforms and lunches the night before ensures our days run smoother and are less hectic. Personally, I find clutter and unwashed dishes irritating, so I always go to bed with a fairly clean and tidy house knowing that when we wake up our day starts on a good note!

Weekdays are pretty busy, and I'd love to be able to spend more time with the kids during the week or take them to after-school activities. We did actually try after-school activities a while ago, and although we thought it was the right thing to do, the kids were too tired and overstimulated. All they wanted to do was chill out at home and for me to be there. This was a good lesson to not do things just because we think we should, or because other parents do it. If it's not right for us and our situation, then that's okay. Knowing when there is too much going on, or when it feels like there's too much pressure, we know it's time to pull back, take a breath, and think about what's serving a real purpose.

Admittedly, for me, finding and achieving balance is no mean feat when juggling motherhood and work. I'm in Perth, and my family is in the UK, so we can't rely on them on the days when the kids are sick, I need to attend a last-minute meeting, or I need some help with school pick-ups. These are the days when it's hard, and I feel a whole new level of guilt. A family member once said to me that she didn't have children just to put them in childcare and have someone else raise them. She had zero intention of offending me; it was simply her opinion, but I'd be lying if I said it doesn't hang over my head. But—and this is a big but—I'm comfortable with my decision to work, and I'd go as far as saying I am proud to be a working mum. Of course, days can be busy and difficult, and we get tired, but for me, being a non-working parent isn't an option. During times when I wasn't working, I felt lost, uninspired, lonely (while never actually being alone), flat, and just a bit empty. I struggled for a long time with questioning if this made me a 'bad mum,' and I can confidently say that it did not. I couldn't love my children more, but I was not able to be my best self because I had no balance, my self-worth was non-existent, and my mental health suffered.

My children's dad, Marty, absolutely devotes himself to them. He is present, plays with them, reads to them, loves them, and would do anything for them. However, I must admit that the sharing of parental responsibilities isn't equal, and I'm not sure it ever will be. This isn't due to any intentional or ill-mannered choice on Marty's part, but rather a societal, underlying, unconscious expectation that, as the mother, I am the one who works things out when someone is unwell or when juggling daycare/school drop-offs. This is also influenced by the nature of our respective work. As a tradesperson, Marty has longer daily work hours than I do, with early starts, weekend work, and unpaid time off.

My role allows for greater flexibility and provides for paid carers leave when needed, which I am definitely very grateful for. But I do question whether this is fair at times, with typical gendered stereotypical roles placing higher importance on "masculine" professions with less benefits that align with family values. My work is important too, and the juggle can cause frustration and stress at times. But, as I've said, it is my choice to be a full-time working mum, and here is where the loop back to removing pressure and high expectations becomes important. A fundamental and crucial point to note here is that communication is key. Since talking more about the 'juggle struggle', Marty is happily and actively playing a greater role in the daycare/school drop-offs and pick-ups, something both he and the children love!

Returning to work after becoming a parent has been, and continues to be, an emotional roller-coaster, and I have had mixed experiences. I am currently in a role that I love! It challenges me and provides me with room for growth while also allowing me the space to be a mum who is present for her children. Flexibility is key, as is working with a supportive manager who accepts—and encourages—that my priority will always be my children. This relationship allows me to alleviate any guilt from both being an employee and a mum who needs to be working from home because I have a sick child. In return, I am loyal, committed, motivated, eager, and engaged. I want to do my job and do it well. Working for a supportive and understanding employer brings that out even more. But not all work environments are this progressive. A less-than-supportive past employer would call me if I wasn't online at 8:02am, questioning where I was, if I even wanted to work, and suggesting that perhaps I should take a role that was "a bit easier for someone in your position." I was two minutes late because, well, parenting, but let's not forget the two hours of unpaid overtime I did the evening prior. For obvious reasons, I left that job.

Controversially, I do think that when returning to the workplace as a new mum, there may be some roles that may not fit the same. And again, that's okay. I absolutely advocate for women in the workplace; that goes without saying. And I could talk for days on the benefits of supporting women in the workplace. However, in my opinion, it's for the working mum to consider their own personal situation and whether a role is going to work for them and their employer. I am fortunate that at present my role allows for flexibility; it allows for me to work from home a couple of days a week, which in turn, enables me to enjoy dropping my children off to school in the morning instead of out-of-school care. Without this flexibility, my stress and anxiety levels would be a lot higher. For me, trying to get myself and two children ready and out the door before 7:00am is tough and significantly contributes to me feeling overwhelmed and guilty.

This leads me to the conclusion of my chapter, which, upon reflection, feels a bit like a therapy session—in a good way! It is difficult to provide advice to a mum who is considering returning to work or to someone already back at work and struggling with aspects of being a working parent. This is because the very nature of parenthood is so personal, individual, and unique. Everyone's situation is different. All I can say is that, in my personal opinion, if a mum is feeling like she wants to return to work but feels guilty about making this decision, she should stop and take the time to assess why. Take time to think about what you want, why you want it, how you feel right now, and how going back to work could make you feel. How is your well-being, and what are your needs? As a mum, I feel like we get so caught up in looking after and caring for everyone else's needs that we neglect our own. It's important to be honest with yourself, prioritise yourself, and care for yourself.

Being a working mum, in my experience, isn't easy, but that doesn't mean it isn't worth it. My well-being has improved significantly, and I am proud of how my children have responded to me being back at work. I have undergone a lot of self-reflection, set boundaries with myself and with others, and learned to let go of unrealistic expectations. It's not about having it all; it's about having all that is important to me and my children. I hope that as my children get older, they see that being a parent doesn't mean putting your life on hold or letting go of what you enjoy and are passionate about. I am a mum, first and foremost, but I am also Kerry McNamee: a person, a friend, a sister, a daughter, and a Human Resources professional who truly loves her job. I am a long way off from being the best version of myself, but I do know that returning to the workplace after becoming a mum gave me back some of my self-worth, self-confidence, joy, and my purpose. My well-being matters, just as much as my children's, and by looking after myself, ultimately, I am looking after them too.

CARLA LOMBARDO

> WHEN WE CONSTANTLY STRIVE TO LIVE UP TO THE PERFECT IMAGE OF 'BALANCE', WE OFTEN END UP DISAPPOINTING OURSELVES. INSTEAD, I'VE ADOPTED THE TERM 'BLENDING' OVER BALANCING.

Carla is a mother, entrepreneur, traveller, and a wellness ambassador on a mission to normalise well-being. She believes the ocean is medicine, hard copy books are healing, and travel is the best education.

CARLA LOMBARDO

AUTHOR NAME: CARLA LOMBARDO
BUSINESS NAME: EAGLE & OWL
POSITION: FOUNDER
BUSINESS INDUSTRY: PERSONAL DEVELOPMENT
WEBSITE: WWW.EAGLEANDOWL.COM.AU
INSTAGRAM: @EAGLE.AND.OWL
INSTAGRAM: @CARLAJLOMBARDO

INTRODUCTION

In the past, I had privately judged some women I knew and even those I didn't, questioning their choices as working mothers with childcare assistance. I thought, "Why are they entrusting someone else with their child's care?"

There was a time when ignorance had a firm grip on my understanding. Ignorance, I now know, is far from bliss; it carries the seeds of destruction. The turning point came when I chose to expand my mind, embracing knowledge, conducting research, and listening to others. This shift allowed me to recognise and take advantage of opportunities that life presented, advocating for healthier ways of living, and discarding the shackles of misinformation that once held me back. With this new outlook, the most dangerous thought to me became the prospect of living an unfulfilled life.

Purpose often emerges from the depths of adversity, as it did for me. Over time, my purpose has grown and evolved, shaping itself with every step of personal development and every success I've achieved because I continue to expand my mind.

There is always a better way to 'do life.' I write this chapter with the intention to plant the seeds for you to absolutely thrive in this life. This is a testament to my mission of normalising well-being. It's also a tale of a mother's love and powerful lessons that transformed me from a conformist to a dream-chaser, and it's now the love I have for myself as a mother and the love I give as a mother. May this inspire you to embrace your unique journey and fulfill your heartfelt desires.

REFLECTING ON CHILDHOOD

My parents owned a business that my sister and I helped working in, a charming wedding reception lounge and motel, jointly owned and operated by my parents. My sister and I have many fond memories of this time. There's one particular moment that stands out, it was one morning after a wedding. As we diligently cleaned up the venue and prepared it for the next celebration, my sister and I engaged in a delightful competition. Racing against time, we eagerly collected any cash that had slipped from guests' pockets, back when physical currency was the norm.

As children, we learn by observing. I observed my parents working hard, not just your regular hard, but around the clock, all-consuming hard. Watching them, at a young age, I decided I never wanted to own a business.

Life's scales seemed to tip towards one direction in my early years, forming a negative mental attitude influenced by various factors. Everyone always told me, "Life is hard." The media and news, well-meaning yet limiting beliefs of my grandparents, and the generational traumas borne by my father all contributed to a fear-based outlook on life. Such contrast to the fearless and extraordinary attitude my mother embodied.

Nevertheless, the seeds of her courage were sown within me, albeit blossoming a little later than anticipated.

My mother has always been endlessly encouraging and supportive of any endeavour I undertake. Her unwavering belief in me and her profound philosophy on life have been guiding lights throughout my journey. She instilled in me the courage to explore new paths, seize opportunities, and pursue my wildest dreams.

Growing up, I encountered the societal norms that dictated a rigid set of rules to follow: excel academically, attend university, secure a stable job with benefits, marry, and start a family. I wasn't interested in conforming to these rules or this timeline, yet I still dutifully aspired to be a "good member of society."

My mother empowered my sister and me to nurture curiosity and discover the passions that ignited our souls. We were given the freedom to pave our own paths and turn our individual dreams into reality, not her dreams. While it took me some time to find my true calling, I eventually embraced the journey of self-discovery and emerged as a late bloomer in the grand symphony of life.

EMBRACING A NEW ROLE

Before becoming a mother, I never had a clear vision of my future. My partner attempted multiple times to discuss finding something of interest for myself—like a hobby or a business idea—before motherhood. He feared that my sense of purpose would fade away once our child arrived, leaving me feeling lost and unfulfilled. While I knew he meant well, his perspective infuriated me.

I couldn't understand why liking my job wasn't enough for him. Back then, I loved my job at Virgin Australia and those international airport vibes! Yet my self-doubts limited my ambition, even though deep down I wanted more. My partner saw untapped potential in me that I couldn't see in myself. He believed I was capable of so much more, but I felt content to play it safe and settle for the life I knew.

As motherhood approached, I found myself internally battling with the concept of being a working mother. Society's expectations led me to believe that staying home to care for my child was what we were meant to do, but I also should be working because women need to "do it all", and with the economic climate, how can a household survive on one wage?

I was excited for that special first year of motherhood, where I could enjoy guilt-free and stress-free moments with my little one. Then reality hit. That first year of being a new mum was a rollercoaster of emotions: magical, scary, empowering, sad, easy, hard, exciting, and frustrating all at once. And when the toddler stage arrived, yikes! I wanted to run in the opposite direction. But I was stuck, just the two of us, with COVID lockdowns and meltdowns aplenty.

I knew it was time for me to ditch society's rules and embrace my own happiness. And if you're reading this and feeling the same way I did, then this is your sign to just go for it! Whether you need a break from just being a 'mum,' financial security, enjoyment, or to become an entrepreneur, this is your permission to do what's right for you.

Now, being a working mother aligns with my goals of creating the life I desire, instilling healthy habits in my household. I get to show my children a better way to do life, teaching valuable lessons from my own experiences that go way beyond what is learned in school.

CONQUERING MOTHERHOOD'S TRIALS

In my motherhood journey, I faced common challenges, but I realised that "common" doesn't mean "normal," and nor should we accept it as normal. You can accept or reject any idea that comes forth.

I dealt with gut health issues, post-partum pain, extreme tiredness (not from sleepless nights—my baby slept through the night from five months old), stress and anxiety, mood swings, resentment, anger, guilt, shame, and a host of negative emotions.

The most significant challenge came when I suffered a stroke. My baby had just turned one.

Panicked about my situation—surviving on one income (especially after 12 months of maternity leave)—along with my ongoing recovery and relentless negative thoughts made me want to give up. Battling these thoughts drained me, leaving little energy for healing, motherhood, or my partner. That's not the life I wanted for myself or my family.

To overcome these hurdles, I focused on transforming my thoughts. I dove into personal development, discovering fears, and re-evaluating my belief system.

I taught myself how to remove a negative thought and replace it with a positive one. I gained a whole new level of self-love, mastered a whole new level of self-confidence, and discovered forgiveness is critical to setting yourself free.

There's no easy answer; I had to do the internal work all on my own. No one was coming to save me; I had to change for my life to change. So, I started with, "What do I want?" It was so difficult and I had no idea what I wanted from life! Asking myself this seemingly mundane question mattered; it set me on the path of transformation and growth.

EMPOWERED MINDSET

Embracing my situation and how I wanted to view the world was a choice. I started to see obstacles as opportunities, and I started my own business! Yep, the very thing I didn't want as a young child.

I quickly understood the need to cultivate an entrepreneurial mindset: always thinking differently, viewing things differently, and investing in myself to support this mindset.

I invest in myself in three main ways:

Engaging in business courses, conferences, and retreats.

Enrolling in personal development programs.

Prioritising my health and well-being, which means unapologetically taking care of myself.

Now, let's get to the core of the matter: the secret formula for success.

First, you want to define your top five personal values. Mine are Health and Well-being, Experiences, Gratitude, Peace, and Happiness. They essentially define the essence of my life, however, they may change over time as I evolve as a person. Knowing my values feeds my mindset. Every action I take must fit into one of my top five values; if it doesn't fit, it's not right for me. This is part of the secret formula for success: discover your values.

Secrets are perilous in our world. Openness and trust are key to healthy relationships (even the relationship with yourself), ensuring we can protect and guide each other without shadows of secrecy.

When we share our information to grow, rise, and succeed together, we contribute to a better society and raise the consciousness of humanity.

THE BLENDING ACT

I've learned that balance is unattainable. When we constantly strive to live up to the perfect image of "balance", we often end up disappointing ourselves. Instead, I've adopted the term "blending" over balancing. As a wise mentor once told me, "It's about blending all aspects of life rather than aiming for a perfect balance."

I've experienced countless moments of 'mum guilt' where I've had to sacrifice family time to improve and grow professionally. Planning my days meticulously, only to see them disrupted when my four-year-old son is at home, can lead to frustration. There are times when I feel like letting out a scream, Hulk-style!

Finding the right blend involves experimentation, and each new challenge (read: opportunity) requires adjustments. With time, I've become better at navigating through it.

The best part is that I get to take my son on this journey with me and involve him. He joins me in my business meetings, sits at the table, and we give him our full attention and ask for his opinion (whether it makes sense or not is irrelevant). We discuss money openly, removing any fear associated with it as a dirty word, and we create a vision of the future together. We even make vision boards together!

SUPPORT NETWORK

Support comes in different forms. With an immensely supportive partner, he held the fort during the gruelling healing journey (at the time of writing this, I have been healing from a stroke for 3.5 years). At some points, we were just barely surviving on one income. We had the ultimate head start in our funds getting extremely depleted, and whatever we had went towards my health because I cannot be replaced.

We had to get extremely creative to think of ways to financially support our family unit. When you're at the bottom of the barrel and forced to problem-solve, it's actually a good thing!

Support also looks like this: me telling my partner what I need because he definitely is not a mind-reader. When I need time out, he always provides me with the space I need.

When it comes to hands-on help, well, my mum lives five hours drive south. My partner lost his parents when he was a child, so it's just us. My amazing mum comes to help when she can, but for the most part, it's just us.

My friendships began to change because I had changed, and their worlds changed too. Babies were added, priorities shifted, and the support system of a friendship group that we once knew was difficult to carry over to the new world. I found a new support network online through social media, podcasts, and books, which led me to find like-minded people and build a new circle of influence.

It's tough, I get it. Yet I know everything always works out the way it's meant to. Staying united as a couple, even when everything feels like it's falling apart, and not turning on each other is true support.

NAVIGATING THE WORKING PARENT JOURNEY

When I had a stroke in 2020, I couldn't work, even if I wanted to. Not working riddled me with guilt! My manager at the time was so incredibly understanding, soothing me with her kindness in such a dark time.

My work ethic has always been so solid that I thought taking a sick day or mental health day was detrimental to my work. I didn't want to let my team down, but in turn, I let myself down.

Then COVID hit, and circumstances changed. I was forced to make a quick decision about the job I loved: choose redundancy or hang in there and hope I get better quickly and hope that they see me as a valuable employee, so I don't potentially end up losing my job without compensation. I laugh now because I can see how trivial this "choice" was, yet it felt so monumental at the time.

I see very clearly now that the situation was created to benefit me, forging a new path, although, at the time, it was terrifying not being able to see the road ahead.

It can be isolating to feel that no one understands what you're going through, whether it be from ill health, stepping into 'matrescence' for the first time, or starting a new business and having no clue what to do. You never need to justify your actions or feelings; you just need to back yourself. People will judge you no matter which step you take, don't waste precious energy on low vibrational emotions like worry, self-doubt, or fear.

Navigating this new journey requires the practice of awareness and being in the right state, a "beautiful state" as Tony Robbins calls it. When you are in this state, you are vibrating at a higher frequency, which means your immunity is stronger, you attract more of what you want into your life, and you have the right attitude to deal with anything that comes your way.

RETURNING TO WORK

I was always such a worrywart. As maternity leave came to an end, my manager at Virgin Australia asked me to return earlier than expected because they had changed the back-to-work training dates. Me being me, wanting to be the good employee, said, "Sure, no problem." But it was a huge problem. I hadn't even put my child on a single childcare waiting list because, well, I wasn't too sure about this whole childcare thing.

Oh my, I stressed myself out so much I could feel my internal organs ache. As the back-to-work date loomed closer, this newfound anxiety was through the roof.

Childcare is a mixed bag of emotions for me. Let's face it, it's rare to find educators who share the exact same values, beliefs, and behaviours as you. Yet it can be a place of fun, laughter, learning, and friendship. I needed daycare! I couldn't look after my son on my own all day, and I wasn't able to give him the stimulation or environment he needed for growth and development.

I worried about sending my son to daycare for such long hours. Was he being cared for properly? Was he being fed the right things? Did he have a proper nap? That first day was one of the longest days of my life. I felt terrible! But I needed the help, I needed the rest, and I needed time to heal and focus my attention on creating a business. Some days he would cry when I dropped him off, some days I would cry longer than he did. Eventually, he (we) got used to it; he made friends and enjoyed it. Childcare was a lifesaver for me! I am so grateful to all those wonderful humans who look after other people's children, and especially those who looked after mine.

One of the misguided teachings of our Western culture is that multitasking makes you a superhero. You might have heard the saying, "If you need something done, give it to a busy mother." Statements like this place unrealistic expectations on women. If you ask for help, you're the failure. If you try to do it all, like your mother and grandmother, then you're sacrificing your health and happiness in the process. We need to normalise taking care of ourselves first to take care of everything else, and if that means utilising resources like daycare or a nanny, then do it.

In the past, I used to boast about being a multitasker, believing it was a valuable skill that made me more desirable to an employer. But as a reformed multitasker, I now know the opposite to be true. I've learned to focus on one task at a time, and surprisingly, I achieve more with efficiency and accuracy than when I used to split myself across multiple tasks simultaneously.

You don't have to do it all (at once), and you can have it all.

You'll find your groove and a routine that suits your family. The challenging times never last forever if you see they are just opportunities in disguise.

CONCLUSION

I love that I get to be a mother. I get to nourish and nurture my family. I get to choose my standards and what I accept in my life. I know so many beautiful women who are incredible mothers, selflessly dedicating themselves to their children and others, giving every last drop.

Personally, I am an advocate for blending, not burnout. There is a lot of light-hearted 'lols' on social media about being a burnt-out mother, which normalises something that shouldn't be normalised. Take care of yourself first. When you make time for yourself, you'll show up as the best version of yourself at home, at work, and in relationships. You cannot be replaced, but your job can, and your job can also replace you. You are your most important asset, choose and love yourself wholeheartedly.

I liken the entrepreneurial path to motherhood; it does take a village. You can do it by yourself, yet everything takes 10 times longer; it's harder, you make lots of mistakes, you cry a lot, and it can be depleting. But when you have your village to support you, it makes life better. You get things done quicker, you receive guidance (less crying), and you can even learn better ways to do things. If you've got your village, ask them for help (if you need it). If you don't have a village—find one, that's what I did.

We are all such powerful beings, especially as women. Sometimes all it takes is discovering that you have this inherent strength; the next step is to unleash your full potential.

LISA YOUNGER

> UNTIL YOU REALLY SEE YOURSELF AS WORTHY OF ALL THOSE THINGS, MOTHERHOOD IS GOING TO BE HARD BECAUSE IT TAKES A LOT OF TIME, ENERGY, MONEY, AND EMOTIONAL STRENGTH TO BE ABLE TO SUPPORT ANOTHER LITTLE HUMAN. YOU MUST BE GOOD AT TAKING CARE OF YOURSELF AND MAKING YOUR NEEDS A PRIORITY.

Lisa Younger is a Human Resources specialist with over a decade of experience in various corporate roles and industries. Lisa has a Post Graduate Certificate in Human Resources as well as an ICF accredited coaching qualification and Certificate IV in training and assessment. Lisa utilises her skills to provide leadership training, mentoring, and coaching to help managers and business owners effectively inspire and motivate their teams. Lisa has a passion for people which have led her to start her own business in 2019 with a focus on people and performance called Evolving Doors. Lisa specialises in empowering leaders to create engaging, collaborative, and empathic work practices. Lisa's vision is to help business leaders purposefully to create work environments that recognise and reward contribution and create fulfilment through shared achievement.

LISA YOUNGER

NAME: LISA YOUNGER
ROLE: DIRECTOR
ORGANISATION: EVOLVING DOORS
LINKEDIN: LINKEDIN.COM/IN/LISAYOUNGER

SARAH:
Would you be kind enough to start off by telling me a little bit about your background, how you were raised, and how that has shaped the way that you parent as well?

LISA:
I'm Canadian, but my parents are English and came from a generation where "children were not often seen and heard". Both had strict upbringings where there wasn't a lot of room for self-expression, setting your own boundaries, or getting your own needs met. Therefore, while my parents were very loving and much less strict than their parents were, I still felt like my feelings were not meant to be shared and that it was better to just do as you were told rather than try to fight the system. I think this led to me being a people pleaser most of my life. I think when I became a parent, I suddenly realised how hard it is to try to make everyone happy because children have a lot of high needs that are impossible to meet at all times. It is quite a relentless task. You can't be perfect for them all the time and do everything, which for me led to a state of burnout. I started out my career as a Montessori teacher

and I thought I was a bit of a child whisperer. I thought I knew all about how to parent because I was very skilled at managing children's behaviour in a classroom. I think I was overly confident. I think I was good at being a teacher, but it's not the same thing as parenting. Looking after someone else's children is nothing like looking after your own. When I became a parent, I found the relentless nature of the emotional demand very challenging, and that was probably because I hadn't learned how to express my feelings in a healthy way and be heard by others, which left me ill equipped to do the same for my children.

SARAH:
Can you tell us a little bit about your children? I know they have needs. How have you coped with that?

LISA:
I think to parent effectively, you really must know yourself well, know what your limitations are, know what you're comfortable with, and be able to trust yourself. It probably led me closer to what I do now because it's very intertwined with my work. I do often compare leadership to parenting because there are a lot of parallels. You are a leader when you are a parent. You're dealing with very small, irrational people, but they are still people with feelings and minds and need love, respect, and care, which is really the same thing when you are at work. The skills do transfer nicely. I've had clients say to me, "Wow, this coaching has really helped me as a father/mother," which is so nice to hear. I've had to really develop my own emotional intelligence. I've had to learn how to develop my ability to speak my own needs and request support and help. And I've had to develop myself to be able to sit in a mess and be okay with it. When my children are upset, I now know how to handle it without it creating stress for me. It has been an important development for myself, and it's probably made the biggest difference with my children. I've always been

nice and caring as a mother, but my ability to hold space for a lot of big emotions wasn't there in the beginning.

Both my children have challenges. My son is on the autism spectrum and has a medical condition called Cystic Fibrosis (CF), while my daughter was diagnosed with selective mutism when she was five. She is still learning to express herself freely in public environments and often suffers from social anxiety. Both have high needs in different ways, and this has also motivated me to learn a lot to support them in the best possible way. I have done parenting courses, asked other mothers for advice, and done a lot of personal development to work on myself.

SARAH:
When did you go back to work after you had your children?

LISA:
After my first child, Joshua was born, I went back to work quickly, about six months after the birth. I started working one or two days a week in the office, then I worked a day at home. I had great flexibility at the time, and I also had a nanny, as well as my mother-in-law who came to my house each week. I had good care on the days I wasn't there, which made it so much easier. I feel that, for me personally, I needed the balance and diversity in my life to feel happy and engaged. Being at home all the time with small children was quite exhausting and not stimulating enough for me. I'm very envious of women who can stay home all day with their children and remain joyful despite the hard work involved, I think that is beautiful. While I had joyful moments, I found it more hard work being with them full time at home. In my case, work created a balance that made me feel happier and calmer, with that mix of concentrated one-on-one time with the kids and getting out of the house to do something for myself.

SARAH:

Other than understanding your own emotional intelligence, which you've outlined and I'm sure many will really relate to, what would you say the biggest challenge was in terms of being a working mum?

LISA:

There was definitely guilt, for sure. Due to my son's CF, putting him into childcare was potentially harmful to his health due to exposure to illnesses. The first year, he was sick all the time, and that wore on my conscience. I felt like I should really be at home, but at the same time, we couldn't financially afford for me not to work at all. It was something we had to do but it did worry me constantly. However, now I look back on it, it was fine. It fortunately hasn't had any negative impacts on his health long term. It was a choice I had to make when we moved to Perth. I couldn't bring my nanny with me from Adelaide, nor my mother-in-law, I lost my entire support network, which was very difficult. We arrived when I was six months pregnant and I had a lot of challenges ahead: a toddler with special needs, a daughter that didn't sleep, and no support system at all. It was probably one of the hardest years of my life, to be honest. In hindsight, I wish I had been more self-aware of how I was eroding as a person psychologically and physically. But I kept telling myself, "You're fine, you'll be fine, you can do this, you'll be right." That whole mind-over-matter approach, but it didn't work. Eventually, I became unwell and had to go to a GP, and get some intervention and medication for my anxiety, which had turned into depression. I was sleep-deprived, had a toddler with special needs, and a difficult baby with colic who cried all day long and didn't sleep at night. It's common for women to spiral downwards and we often wait far too long to get the help we need.

SARAH:

That sounds really hard! If you were to go back in time, is there anything that you would do differently?

LISA:

Yeah, absolutely. I would have sat my husband down and said to him, "This is serious. I'm not coping. I need help. We need to come up with a Plan B because the current circumstance is not working for me, and I'm concerned for my health." I didn't express it to him clearly enough, and he didn't understand. I was obviously trying to be brave and strong and hide it from others, but in doing that, all I did was make it harder for myself. So, again, it was that vulnerability piece. I wasn't willing to step into my vulnerability and say, "I am not coping; I need help." And even when I did, I went to the GP over my own husband. It's a real indication of where I was on my journey, which was not being able to ask for what I need and put myself as a priority over others. I wasn't giving myself the self-care that I deserved at that stage of my life.

SARAH:

When did you go back to work after your daughter, how did you manage that after what you had been through mentally?

LISA:

It was about 14 months. I took a role that was much less challenging. I was in engineering, and I scaled back, taking a part-time role that I felt was very easily managed.

SARAH:

Did you take that step back career-wise because you felt like you couldn't cope with it?

LISA:

Yeah, I was scared. I was scared that I wouldn't be able to cope, that I wouldn't be able to handle it. It was hard to get the job because they said, "You're overqualified; why do you want to work here?" However, for me, I just needed something where I felt comfortable and that I felt I could handle.

SARAH:

Yeah, I was exactly the same. I totally get it. How long did it take you to build yourself back up after that? Did going back to work help?

LISA:

Yes, it did help. It helped with confidence. That's when I really started the personal development journey and began researching all kinds of things to help me parent more effectively.

SARAH:

And I think that's so important with children as well because they end up becoming a reflection of you, right? So, you being the best version of yourself is the best thing you can do for your children. I'm glad that you started going on that journey. When did you start your own business? How old were your children?

LISA:

My daughter was in kindy and my son was in Year 1, and I thought, "If I'm going to do this, I've got to do it now." I strategically started it mid-year of kindy, thinking that by the time I got busy, they would both be in school full-time. By the end of the six months, I was going great, and I could align all my aftercare and everything for the following year. It worked out quite well.

SARAH:

And what inspired you to start your own business? Was it wanting that flexibility, or was it something that you just wanted to do yourself for your own personal and professional growth?

LISA:

It was a bit of both. In my last role I wasn't aligning with my national General Manager and some of the philosophies around performance management that he was applying. I felt that good leadership practices were not widely practiced across industries and there was an opportunity to make a positive difference in workplaces. People often don't intend to do the wrong thing by their employees, but they don't know how to do it more effectively. A kind of fire erupted in me, and this became something I really wanted to do to make a difference in business. Also, in that same year my son had gotten sick, and he'd been in the hospital for two weeks. It was heartbreaking because I had to keep leaving him to go to work. I didn't know at the time what the trajectory for his medical condition would look like, but I wanted the flexibility to be able to stay with him and not have to leave his side when he was unwell. That was really important to me. In summary, it was a combination between a passion that I've had for years and wanting the flexibility to be there for my son.

SARAH:
Absolutely. Did you ever speak to your boss at the time to say, you know, my child is in the hospital, can I work from home? Or was it just not an option at the time?

LISA:
Oh, look, that's the people pleaser in me. If I had asked, there probably was some flexibility, but this was pre-COVID when businesses believed you couldn't be effective whilst working from home. At the time when my son was in hospital, I'd get the call each day asking, "Are you coming in tomorrow?" Yes, I felt a pressure that made me uncomfortable. I thought that would probably be the case in any workplace, where there would be an unspoken vibe that you knew they were thinking, "This isn't great for us, that you're not coming in." And that's the nature of HR, it's a very hands-on kind of job. People want you there.

SARAH:
Yeah, that makes total sense. If you were to give advice to other

mums out there, what would your advice be in terms of being a working parent?

LISA:

Well, I think to do both—parent and work—you really need to have good structures in terms of how everything's going to get done. You need to map it out. You need to map out all the tasks that you're going to do and all the tasks your partner's going to do, because otherwise it doesn't work. The traditional model doesn't work where the mum does everything. That leads to major burnout, stress, and mental health issues. It's fundamental that, before you are pregnant, you're sitting down with your partner and discussing how things will work, in one year, two years, three years from now. Plan out everything from conversations around childcare to domestic chores to how much time you will have to go to the gym and do yoga or whatever it is that you need for self-care.

I'm now proactive in getting those boundaries in place. If you haven't set boundaries, you can get really stressed out and communicate in ways that are reactive and unkind. This happened to me at times when I was angry about how much of the mental load I was carrying. It was never a great delivery, and all that happened was my husband was left feeling like he was failing and inadequate. It crushed him. It's much better if you can ask in a respectful way before you have hit your breaking point. If you assume that they will automatically know what you need this will likely lead to disappointment. Therefore, we must learn to clearly define and communicate our needs.

SARAH:

Yeah, it's an educational piece as well, right? Because we're still in that generation where our parents and partner's parents probably still have that model of 'women do everything and men don't', so they've got no role models to guide them. So, you must become that for them.

LISA:

Yes exactly. The more you can set it up ahead of having children, before there are problems, the better it works. You need to be aligned as a team and then there's no demand or unreasonable expectation put on anyone. Being well-planned, I think, is important, and don't overestimate what you can do. Get yourself a cleaner, get your food delivered, do whatever you need to do, but don't be a martyr and do too much.

SARAH:

That's really good advice. Is there anything else, any final words of advice that you want to give, Lisa? You've given so much. It's been very, very inspiring to hear from you.

LISA:

I think if you struggle with confidence issues or feel under accomplished or you don't inherently really like yourself, go get some therapy and work on that before you become a mother. Until you are in a position where you can look in the mirror and say, "I'm awesome and I deserve to have time for myself, I deserve to be able to spend money on myself or exercise or have my own free time". Until you really see yourself as worthy of all those things, motherhood is going to be hard because it takes a lot of time, energy, money, and emotional strength to be able to support another little human. You must be good at taking care of yourself and making your needs a priority. It's like the safety briefing when travelling on a plane, "Put your own oxygen mask on before you assist your child." Take care of you and make sure you're in a good place. Know and love yourself before choosing to become a parent.

ASHLEY McGRATH

> I WON'T LIE; IT CAN BE A SH*T SHOW TRYING TO HERD THE CHILDREN OUT THE DOOR WITHOUT THEM LOOKING LIKE THEY ARE HOMELESS, FORGETTING SOMETHING, OR LEAVING THE HOUSE LOOKING LIKE A BOMB SITE, ALL WHILE TRYING TO MAKE YOURSELF PRESENTABLE.

Ashley McGrath is a gender equity trailblazer on a mission to turn the dial in Western Australia and beyond. Ashley leads CEOs for Gender Equity, a for-purpose organisation that seeks to accelerate gender equity by inspiring and supporting CEOs to take action. Ashley is also working on a PhD project that will increase female inclusion and diversity in the Western Australian mining industry.

ASHLEY McGRATH

AUTHOR NAME: ASHLEY MCGRATH
BUSINESS NAME: CEOS FOR GENDER EQUITY
POSITION: CHIEF EXECUTIVE OFFICER
BUSINESS INDUSTRY: FOR-PURPOSE/NON-FOR-PROFIT
WEBSITE: WWW.CEOSFORGENDEREQUITY.COM.AU
SOCIAL MEDIA/ LINKEDIN USER NAME:
LINKEDIN: LINKEDIN.COM/IN/ASH-MCGRATH

THE EXPERIENCE THAT SHAPED ME

Fulfilling. That's the best word I can think of to describe my childhood. It wasn't the most straightforward, but my gosh, did I learn from every twist and turn. My mum was a relief teacher which was a perfect match for her warm and compassionate nature. She is also anxious and neurotic. This combined with the uncertain and urgent nature of the relief profession unfortunately resulted in Mum having a mental breakdown in 1992. I was five. I hadn't really thought about it until writing this chapter, but I am sure that experience primed my unwavering awareness of a work/life blend. Mum never returned to work, but my brother and I reaped the benefits of her love, nurture, and support in our upbringing.

My dad built a phenomenal career in leadership in the aerospace manufacturing industry. He worked his butt off six days a week to provide our family with a beautiful home, a comfortable lifestyle, and annual overseas family holidays where we made priceless memories. He was also very hands on raising my brother and I, taking us on countless adventures and teaching us important life lessons through deep conversations. We would often discuss his work and how he was overcoming challenging situations. I always admired his confidence, tenacity, and dedicated work ethic.

In 2005, when I was 18, my parents amicably separated and later that year Dad got the devasting news that he had aggressive prostate cancer and that the outlook wasn't good. I am delighted to report that 18 years later, he is a pillar of health! He never returned to work after treatment, and now spends his days helping others.

My brother followed in my dad's footsteps, building a successful career in the same aerospace organisation. He also mirrors my dad's love for his family and plays a very active role in the raising on his three children.

I feel like I really got the best of both worlds with my parents. I look up to them both in different ways and believe myself as a blend of both of their best bits!

WHY WORK?

Being a working mum means the world to me, especially in my current role as CEO of an organisation that accelerates gender equity. I've learned that my social purpose is my motivator, knowing that my work leads to better outcomes for people of all genders drives me to do more, be more, and achieve more.

Besides loving my job, there are many more reasons why I will always be a working mum. I was raised to be independent, understand the value of money, and always have savings for the unexpected. I thought my dad was like Superman, being able to thrive in his career while providing physical, mental, and financial support for our family. I don't mind admitting that I didn't aspire to work as hard as my dad, who worked six days a week with plenty of overtime. I knew the toll it took on him, even though he never complained. My mum still speaks fondly of her teaching days, and although I can't remember much from when she was a working mum, I know she would have excelled at it.

I have three kids: two sons aged six and seven, Mason and Maverick, respectively, and a stepdaughter who is 15, Katelyn. I went back to work part-time when both my sons were five months old, so being a working mum is all they have ever known. When my stepdaughter came into my life, I was working full-time and completing my PhD part-time. I wanted to show my kids that it's possible to raise a family, have a happy marriage, enjoy an awesome social life, stay fit, and flourish in your career. I wanted to inspire them to pursue a job they love and not let parenthood, or anything else, get in the way of chasing their dreams. From a practical perspective, I have been able to provide for my kids, even during the period of being a single working mum. If I hadn't been a working mum, I might not have been able to leave my first marriage. It was tough, but thanks to the career I had built, I could afford my own place and raise my boys while working part-time. I will be forever grateful for that.

WORKING MUM CHALLENGES AND HOW TO COPE
AVAILABILITY OF QUALITY DAYCARE

I always secured daycare close to home as opposed to work as it's more effective logistically. Do your research and ask for recommendations from your mums' group/friends in the area. You will also need to plan ahead, depending on the kind of daycare you are after and the area you live in, you may need to get on a waitlist.

COST OF CHILDCARE

If, like in Australia, your government subsidises childcare, ensure you get all your paperwork sorted and set up correctly in advance. Talk to your tax agent about the implications of going back to work and the difference in take-home pay depending on how many days you work.

SICKNESS—IT'S INEVITABLE.

Every parent who sends their kids to daycare, regardless of their age when they start, is hit with a whirlwind of bugs for the first six months. Yes, you will feel frazzled trying to manage it while working, but my kids now have the immune system of an ox. They are very, very rarely sick, unlike some kids who haven't been to daycare.

BEFORE AND AFTER SCHOOL CARE
Once the kids hit school age, you may need to book them into the on-site before and after school care service. My sons go twice a week in the afternoon when I work in the city.

THE MORNING RUSH
I won't lie; it can be a sh*t show trying to herd the children out the door without them looking like they are homeless, forgetting something, or leaving the house looking like a bomb site, all while trying to make yourself presentable. Prepare as much as you can the night before and allow plenty of time in the mornings.

HOMEWORK
We do Maverick and Mason's reading before bed and save other homework for the weekend when things are more relaxed.

DOMESTIC LOAD
Get a cleaner. Do arduous cooking only on weekends. Always pack lunches the night before and consider allowing the kids to go to the canteen on a Friday; you deserve a break from packed lunch monotony!

Remember that where there's a will, there's a way! Don't put up a front on the challenges; openly share them, seek advice, and encourage others to do the same. Us working mums are all in the same boat.

MINDSET
I'm not going to sugar coat it; the 'mum guilt' is real. I get a pang

of it every so often if I can't make an assembly, don't have enough quality time with Katelyn, or rush the boys back home after school when they want to play with their friends. I feel guilty when I am a bit short with them because I am tired from work and study. But I have work or study to do. Above everything, I am still my own person. But, to put things in perspective, I feel guilty about 10% of the time, and 90% is all the positive feelings in the "Why work?" section. The truth is that non-working mums face their own challenges, too. They feel guilty that they aren't contributing financially, that they aren't being good working role models, they lose their confidence, and sometimes even their identity.

My mindset is focused on the positive. I am 100% a better mum because of my work. It fills my professional cup while my husband Troy, kids, family, and friends fill the personal cup. My sons thrived at daycare and are the most social, confident, and easy-going kids I know. Katelyn sees and hears my passion for what I do, and I hope that will inspire her to follow her dreams.

Above all else, I have learned to be kind to myself. To put things in perspective and be proud of what I am achieving, being the best mum, wife, friend, and employee I can be, all while keeping myself sane and having the occasional Netflix binge.

THE BLEND

I don't aim for balance; it's a blend. Sometimes, it's even a hot mess. I became a working mum pre-COVID. I requested and was supported to work from home one day a week out of three. I now work from home two or three days a week and am generally in back-to-back meetings and pop into the office on the other days. Working from home is a game-changer for working parents. It's the time saved getting ready, the time and cost of the commute, the ability to go to my favourite gym class or put on a load of washing. Aside from all this making me happy, it allows me to be more present as a parent, whether it be leisurely walking my kids to school and having morning chats or having the brainpower to really engage at reading time.

I am ridiculously organised with my work. Each day, my calendar is full of meetings and/or my to-do list. If I have a phone call or online meeting with someone I already know, you better believe I am multitasking, walking the dog, riding my bike or folding laundry at the same time. If I am dialled into a conference call or training that doesn't involve me presenting, I am 100% whipping up a batch of spag bol and tidying the house. I plan face-to-face meetings only for my city days unless it is super urgent. I am efficient with my meeting schedule logistically, so I am not doubling back on myself or having to go in and out of the city twice.

I am efficient with everything I do; it helps to manage the blend. Plus, if I'm honest, I get a kick out of it!

SUPPORT

I am a Northern Irish girl. In 2011, when I was 24, I got married and moved to Western Australia to live the dream. I had Mason in 2016 and Maverick in 2017 (there are 15 months between my boys—mad, I know!). All my immediate family—the go-to guilt-free babysitters—are back in Northern Ireland. When you are from another country, your friends become your family, and I am fortunate to have a vast and incredible network. Since the day M&M were born, if anyone said, "Reach out if I can help with babysitting," I would look them dead set in the eye and say, "I am the kind of person who *will* take you up on that, so expect a call!". And so, I did. From a young age, the boys had other people looking after them, at our house or theirs. They would go for endless sleepovers and playdates. When the boys were little, I had friends come and work from my house with my baby asleep on their chest so I could have a nap. One of my old neighbours used to take Mason for one afternoon a week, and it was a godsend. I saw, and still see, other new mums around me struggle, but they don't ask for help. I remind them that it's okay to ask for help! And I pester them until they book in a massage or date night.

I talk loudly and proudly of my openness to help, and I ensure I am proactive in providing support for others. You're wondering why there is no mention of M&M's father, right? That's because he was more of a burden than a help. I'll leave that one there. Three years ago, I met the man of my dreams, Troy, and we recently eloped in the dreamiest beach ceremony. Troy is my rock and the backbone of our blended family. My career has skyrocketed since I met Troy, and he is the most incredible physical and mental support for our family. My advice from all of this? Don't settle for less than your perfect partner, ask for help, embrace help offered, and pay it forward.

A CRASH COURSE IN MY CAREER

When I moved to Western Australia, I continued my career in recruitment, working my way up to a State Sales Manager role by 2015. While in this role, I fell pregnant with Mason. I loved my job, worked for an awesome company with top people, and had a very supportive leader, so it was a no-brainer that I wanted to be a working mum. When Mason was five months old, I came back to work three days a week, with one of those days working from home. Being a working mother came relatively easily to me thanks to working part-time in a familiar role, having a supportive leader, and a job that was flexible in nature. I got such a buzz knowing I had more days off a week than I worked to make memories with Mason and catch up with friends.

I fell pregnant with Maverick when Mason was six months old, and followed the same timeline going back to my career and it worked wonderfully. I even managed to score a promotion while on my second spell of parental leave, which was a powerful experience. When Mason started full-time school, I moved up to four days a week (two from home) and enjoyed 'Maverick and mummy day' every Monday. When Maverick started full-time school, I moved to working five days, keeping two days working from home. The working from home days kept me sane, and I loved getting glammed up to head out on client visits and catch up with my colleagues in the office the other days.

In 2022, I was sponsored into the job of my dreams leading CEOs for Gender Equity. I still work at least two days from home. I start work at 7:00am and smash out an hour before getting the kids organised and walked up to school. I make time for exercise and pick up the boys from school three times a week before finishing off work in the late afternoon. I have been very fortunate to have a career that allows a high degree of flexibility, which has helped my working mum experience immensely.

MY ADVICE

Being a working mum is awesome! Find your passion and craft your career around it. Even if your first step back into the workforce isn't your dream job, it will help you rediscover yourself after the whirlwind of parenthood. It will also help you get a physical and mental break from your kids, build your social network, and gain financial independence. Look for jobs that offer flexibility and a supportive culture. Don't stress if your first 12 months are a bit bumpy; it is for all of us. Be open and honest with your employer about what you need to be a happy working mum. Take all the support that comes your way, and don't be shy about asking for more.

I cannot recommend becoming a working mum enough! My work has always been part of my identity, and I have never felt one bit guilty about pursuing my career for that reason. You go, girl!

NICOLA VEAL

> MY GREATEST ASPIRATION FOR MY SONS IS THAT THEY GROW UP CONNECTED TO THEIR OWN VALUES, DISCOVER THEIR CALLINGS, AND, IN TURN, BECOME SOURCES OF INSPIRATION FOR OTHERS.

Nicola, a dynamic leader in Human Resources, blends innovation with strategic insight to drive transformative change. Holding a Master's Degree in Human Resource Management and a Bachelor of Commerce, her professional journey showcases unwavering commitment to excellence. As a Human Resources Manager, she champions diversity, inclusion, and continuous learning. Beyond boardrooms and conferences, as a mother of two boys and a co-builder of a family farm, she embodies modern motherhood's balance between career and family. Nicola's story reflects resilience, adaptability, and the belief that with passion and purpose, hurdles become stepping stones. Through her journey, she aims to inspire working mothers worldwide to show that the right mindset can help them "have it all."

NICOLA VEAL

AUTHOR NAME: NICOLA VEAL
BUSINESS NAME: NA
POSITION: HUMAN RESOURCES MANAGER
BUSINESS INDUSTRY: HUMAN RESOURCES
WEBSITE: NA
LINKEDIN: LINKEDIN.COM/IN/NICOLA-VEAL

I know it's not what you would expect to see in a book about parenting, but I want to start by admitting that I never thought I wanted children. In fact, when I met my now-husband, I proudly told him I didn't believe in love, marriage, or happily ever afters. As someone who always wanted a family, he took a gamble in choosing to love me. After all, we did meet at a poker game, so I shouldn't have been surprised! Whether it was fate or his cleverly designed plan, I did fall for him. We married in 2018 and now have two beautiful, cheeky sons who I can't imagine my life without.

While I can say our journey was a whirlwind romance, it was not an easy one. We are both career-driven high-achievers with an all-in attitude. Doug, who you can read more about in the book, 'Working Dads and Balancing Acts,' followed a career in Policing, with a recent move to the federal government, whereas I found my love for Human Resources and designing the future of work. We moved quickly—and by that, I mean we relocated to a regional town within just a few months of dating. We raised chickens, rabbits, cats, and dogs before I finally admitted that maybe I wanted kids. But before we get to that part, let me provide you with a bit of background about myself.

I grew up in New South Wales, raised by a single dad. My grandparents played a significant role in my upbringing and are featured in most of my childhood memories. My mum lived a few hours away, and although we only saw her for a weekend between each school holidays, we were often in contact and (with a few exceptions during my sulky teenage years) have always been close.

I have always been creative and entrepreneurial. I watched as my dad left a successful career in mining to be at home with us. He started his own businesses, breaking the absent-father stereotype, and structured his work hours to attend as many award ceremonies and school pick-ups as he could. We spent our weekends visiting his warehouse and office in between soccer games and Girl Guides excursions. We observed and learned how he managed negotiations, projects, and timelines. Every evening, he would be home to cook us dinner, for which I am grateful (even when it was fish—yuck!). He nurtured a love of books and learning in me. As a child, some of the most treasured gifts he gave me were copies of 'To Kill a Mockingbird,' 'Lord of the Flies,' and 'Animal Farm.' Together we explored the works of Da Vinci and the theories of Einstein. The lessons he taught me were more significant than the facts and figures. He taught me to keep learning continuously, which has been pivotal in my life and my career.

Always an achiever, I breezed through most of school. Or at least until I discovered the joys of a social life in my late teens. Going straight to university, I found little joy in my degree. Unsure of what my path should be, I chose a Bachelor of Commerce, thinking a double major in Management and Marketing would get me anywhere I wanted to go—once I figured out where that was. As I threw myself into casual work at an experiential marketing company (as a way to procrastinate completing assignments), I found my vocation: Human Resources. I didn't realise the weight of finding it at the time, and I took much of it for granted.

It's only as it has evolved in the last few years that I have recognised and been grateful for finding it so early in life. I fell into recruitment which, over time, evolved into a love for Human Resources. I continued my studies, completing my Bachelor, then moving on to study my Masters in HR Management, plus a couple of Advanced Diplomas. This paid off as I became the Manager of Human Resources at a multinational, billion-dollar company at the ripe age of 28.

In 2018, I was working for a recruitment agency. It wasn't long after my wedding. I vividly recall having an awful headache, and on the pharmacist's recommendation, I took a pregnancy test before taking the painkillers they suggested. I was sitting in the bathroom at work and shaking as that little pink line appeared. The little pink line that forever shapes your future.

By that time, I had changed my mind about not having children, and although I knew I wanted them, I spiralled into a panic. You see, in my teenage years, I was diagnosed with a moderately-severe subaortic stenosis, which is an unwanted membrane just under my aortic valve. Theoretically, this would have little impact on my life except for a funny sounding heartbeat. However, when it was first diagnosed, my cardiologist told me that if—and when—I became pregnant I may need surgical intervention. Although at my last check-up, he reassured me that I was safe to fall pregnant, the words "surgical intervention" seemed to play on a loop in my mind.

I continued to work full time, studying in the evenings and on weekends. Our prenatal appointments became more regular as the pregnancy progressed, making it difficult to commit to full-time work. My schedule was ruled by cardiologists, ultrasound technicians, midwives, obstetricians, and GPs. Each appointment led to more tests and scans.

At around 22 weeks, working full time became impossible, so I chose to take on temp roles that gave me more flexibility as my pregnancy progressed. The rest of the pregnancy was utter chaos. I would walk from one doctor's office to another. At one appointment, I found out that the medication I had just been prescribed could cause my heart to stop beating. At 26 weeks pregnant, I was told that my son needed to be born immediately. Due to my heart condition, a "cardiac event" was likely to happen during the delivery, and the risk went higher the longer the pregnancy went. The hospital scrambled to send me off to different specialists for a second opinion, and then a third. Ultimately this left us in a position where we would go to our weekly appointment, each time wondering if this was the week our son would be born.

It took three cardiologists with teams from three different hospitals for Edison to be safely born on Christmas Eve—only five weeks early and in front of a team of 27 in the operating theatre. Despite eight long days in the neonatal unit and a case of talipes, he was perfectly healthy, and nothing else mattered.

Whilst I made it through the pregnancy and the caesarean section, it took a large toll on my heart. Our team of medical professionals referred me for an open-heart surgery before we even thought about falling pregnant again. We waited until Edison was nine months old and had finished breastfeeding before we scheduled it for Friday 13th September.

I was still on parental leave as we waited for the big day, and I busied myself with mothering and studying. Despite the exhaustion of looking after an infant, I was determined not to let my career pause for too long. I focused my time on trying to finish my studies and achieve something during the 'break'.

During the pregnancy, Doug's drive to achieve more (and supplement our income) saw him join the Army Reserves. Unfortunately (or fortunately, as I would soon discover), he had to attend blocks of training between Edison's birth and my surgery. I was utterly terrified, not of my impending surgery, but of parenting alone for six weeks at a time. Doug's seemingly natural ease with children had become my safety net. When post-natal anxiety and depression seemed to be taking hold, he would be there, taking night feeds, burping our son, and being an overall amazing natural parent. For me, it seemed to be hard work. I didn't think I could face doing it alone, even for a little while. I know how selfish and short-sighted that may sound, as many people don't have a supportive partner. However, in the moment, all I could think about was how badly I was going to fail him, myself, and most importantly, our son.

I know you came here to read stories about working mothers inspiring others, and I promise I will get to that, but it's important that I cover this moment in my life first.

As Doug boarded the plane to go to his first stint of training, I pulled away from the airport with tears in my eyes. I was sure I was going to mess this up. In some ways, I did. I got angry, and I cried tears of frustration, loneliness, and self-hatred. I cursed him for leaving us—even more so when he wasn't given an opportunity to call home for the first eight days.

It was the week from hell before I started to see the light. It wasn't someone coming to help me, or that my darling child suddenly learned how to sleep through the night, it was a change in me and my mindset.

The light was dim at first. The first sign was when Edison was screaming and crying, and I couldn't figure out why. I felt the frustration and the anger bubbling up inside me. I couldn't figure out how to get him to settle. When Doug is around, I would usually give up and try let him settle our son. Without him around, it was all up to me.

I caught myself methodically working through the baby checklist, you know the one, dirty nappy? Nope. Too hot or too cold? Nope. Hungry? Nope! When I still couldn't figure it out, I paused, took a deep slow breath, and came back with reassurance rather than frustration.

When I next visited my psychologist, I walked in with the biggest smile on my face. I told her that I could do this—that I was born to be a mother! I learned that I am stronger than I knew, and even if parenting doesn't seem to come as naturally to me as it does to Doug, it still comes.

After I recovered from my heart surgery, I returned to work, determined to have it all. I started a contract role with WA Police Force four days a week assisting with recruitment and selection processes. I also started my Master's Degree in Human Resource Management. Doug and I faced new challenges as we juggled daycare and the inevitable bugs that go along with it. As Doug's income was bigger and more stable than mine (plus he worked days, afternoons, and nights), it was often me who managed everything when we got the dreaded "your child is sick" call from the childcare centre. It was a busy time, and for a while, we found our rhythm, so it's fair to say we weren't expecting what happened next.

Between Doug's army training blocks, I fell pregnant again. Without the heart issues looming over us, we were sure this time would be less stressful, and we could find that pregnancy bliss you see in the movies. Between the COVID-19 lockdowns, the sudden removal of a burst appendix, and a strange series of Friday evenings where I seemed to go into labour (I would start contractions as if I started labour, and the hospital would have to chemically stop it), we didn't get the bliss, but we made it through. Terrence was born in November 2020, and our little family was complete.

Again, Doug took parental leave and was home for the first three months with the kids. This time, I was free to go back to work as soon as I was ready. Terrence was two months old when I started working as a Recruitment Consultant in Aged Care. And this is where my journey as a working parent really changed. As I worked, I managed the precarious balance of full-time work, studying, and parenting. For the first few months, I would drive to daycare on my lunch break to feed the baby, I would pump milk in the bathrooms at the office, and when I worked from home, I would be typing with one hand and expressing with the other. My master's degree was coming along, and the more I studied, the more interesting I found it. I was determined to be in HR one day.

Six months into my role, I was presented the opportunity to step into a HR Business Partner role in the small mining town of Kalgoorlie, Western Australia. During this time, Doug was in the middle of being promoted to Sergeant, which meant he would likely be moved to a different spot within the police. I called him, jokingly (and not jokingly) asking if he wanted to move to Kalgoorlie. Without a hint of hesitation, he said, "Yes!"

So, as we started planning the move, he applied for a Kalgoorlie transfer, and I started planning the transition to HR.

Before the official move, I got started in my role by flying in and out of Perth to Kalgoorlie for a fortnight at a time, staying close to the residential aged care facility. I would work in Kalgoorlie Monday-Friday, then fly home every weekend, and every third week I was in the Perth office. Doug would manage the kids at home. We were confident that Doug would get the Sergeant position in Kalgoorlie and the FIFO (fly-in fly-out) life would be a temporary arrangement. So, of course, you can imagine the spanner thrown into the works when he was assigned a role in Perth.

We managed the FIFO life well for a few months. I threw myself into work and loved having time in the evenings to dedicate to my university assignments. When I was home, I was able to be more present and engaging with the boys. Even though we had explained the arrangement to the childcare a thousand times, every sick call would still come to me. It still does, years later. If you're a mum, you know too well about these gendered expectations.

It all became too much when Doug started his master's degree. Although the FIFO life was an interesting experiment, it wasn't sustainable for our family. As a believer that mothers can "have it all", I wasn't going to take a step back in my career. I started looking for a role that would allow me to continue the momentum, while still being home every night to have dinner with the kids.

I am now a Human Resources Manager in a different sector with a myriad of responsibilities. My workday is demanding, especially since I work across multiple time zones, which means it can start and end at unusual times. Doug works full-time in a senior government role while pursuing his master's degree. I've already completed mine, but in addition to working full-time, I'm an active participant and Network Convenor for the Australian HR Institute (AHRI). I'm deeply engaged in my passion, which involves designing the future of work. I also deliver speeches on the impact of generative artificial intelligence on HR and what the future may hold.

For our family, a few key factors have made a significant difference in managing the life of a working mother. However, it's essential to recognise that everyone must discover their own balance. I consider myself fortunate to have an engaged and passionate father as my husband. We both have stable jobs, a lovely home, and supportive families. But I acknowledge that not everyone has the same resources at their disposal or faces the same challenges. Therefore, all I can do is share my experiences and hope it helps in some way!

MANAGING STRESS

Both of us have demanding jobs, each with its unique stressors. We've had to become attuned to recognising when stress is affecting the other and collaboratively find ways to address it as it arises. For instance, when I start to feel overwhelmed and become irritable due to various sources of noise, Doug can discern that I'm getting stressed. In those moments, he steps in to distract the kids and provide me with some space to process my emotions, allowing me to better face the day.

FAMILY CALENDARS

We rely heavily on our calendars, almost religiously. Maintaining a shared family calendar is our cornerstone of organisation. Whenever it appears that one of us may need to travel for work or if there are upcoming events, we block them out on our family calendar. This way, the other person is always aware of our commitments, even if they're still TBC.

SLEEP INS

Taking turns to sleep in on weekends may seem simple, but it's a small joy we look forward to. If one of us has had an exceptionally challenging week, that person gets the first opportunity to sleep in on the weekend. It's remarkable how much easier it becomes to face life's demands after a full night's sleep, even if it's just once a week!

Edison, now four years old, has developed a passion for taekwondo, marking our first venture into Saturday sports. Meanwhile, Terrence, at two, is firmly entrenched in his cheeky but adorable phase. I won't pretend to have everything perfectly aligned, as the notion of "having it all together" seems like a myth to me. Most days we struggle to make it work. We wake up—or are woken up—early and it's go, go, go from start to end. Our primary focus remains on the essentials: ensuring the kids are loved, well-fed, properly dressed, and educated. However, things don't always go according to plan. Sometimes being 'fed' means a lovely meal made from scratch, and sometimes it means cereal for dinner.

Despite experiencing daily moments of self-doubt, I take solace in knowing that my kids are healthy, content, and on track for a bright future. My husband continues to advance in his career and derives fulfillment from his studies, despite the relentless deadlines. As for me, I've wholeheartedly embraced my yearning for continuous learning. I've discovered a career that genuinely resonates with me, where I can witness the positive impact I have on those around me. Each day, I have the privilege of living in alignment with my core values while providing support to my family. My greatest aspiration for my sons is that they grow up connected to their own values, discover their callings, and, in turn, become sources of inspiration for others.

LEISA VAN GEEST

❝

WORKING MUMS ARE NOT SUPERHEROES, AND WE'RE TIRED OF PRETENDING TO BE.

❞

Leisa, a mother of twins, supports Agribusiness clients across a variety of Ag industries in WA. Her unwavering passion lies in helping others navigate their corporate career path, particularly women in business. By openly sharing her experiences, she not only challenges the status quo, but also champions the pursuit of inspiring others to have a fulfilling career with work/life integration.

LEISA VAN GEEST

AUTHOR NAME: LEISA VAN GEEST
BUSINESS NAME: BANKING
POSITION: AGRIBUSINESS EXECUTIVE
BUSINESS INDUSTRY: BANKING & FINANCE
LINKEDIN: LINKEDIN.COM/IN/LEISAVANGEEST
INSTAGRAM: @LEISAVANGEEST

"So how will you handle working full time and having a family?" they asked. I sighed, internally. I was on my third-round interview with key stakeholders of one of the Big Four banks and this was the last interview before they made a hiring decision.

I provided the details of our twin's care roster throughout the week, explained that my husband recently changed his job for more family flexibility and support, and acknowledged that being a working parent is absolutely a balancing act. I also reminded them that if you want something done, give it to someone already busy. If you're a working parent—you know what I mean.

While it felt like the interviewers were impressed, I left the meeting with an 'ick' in my stomach. I couldn't quite put my finger on what it was. I replayed the conversation over and over to try to work out why there was such a difference between how they felt about the meeting and how I felt.

At the most convenient time (right before bed!), a revelation came to me. I was disappointed, I was frustrated, and I was tired.

I was disappointed that I was asked that question. It was

2019—were we not past that?! But I was most disappointed in myself that I had answered it instead of politely shutting it down.

I was frustrated that I had potentially put myself out of the race not knowing if other candidates didn't have, or didn't acknowledge, that they have other commitments (i.e., dependants) outside of work.

And I was tired of feeling like I had to explain how I manage my career and a life as a mum of twins, who at the time were almost two. Tired of then having to have hard conversations that follow, experiencing unconscious—and sometimes conscious—bias because I want to make sure I do what I can as one person to help the world change, so my kids don't experience this when it's their turn.

The next day, I made a proactive call to the recruitment manager, explained my experience, and sought some guidance on how to handle it. They were disappointed to hear about it but encouraged me to contact the hiring manager of the company directly to discuss it. And that's what I did.

The hiring manager asked me how I felt it went, and with a deep breath and shaky hands, I said I felt disappointed. I said that I believed I was asked a question that was not likely posed to all candidates. I felt that if it wasn't a standard question for everyone, it shouldn't have been asked of me. I explained that by answering the question, I felt like I'd put myself at a disadvantage compared to other candidates who might be of a different age, gender, background, or family status.

The hiring manager reflected my view and expressed his own discomfort with the question posed by his colleague. He also conveyed his desire to discuss this matter further. It opened the door for an incredibly candid and honest conversation about the realities of being a working parent, allowed us to talk through the real-life logistics and requirements of the job, and how that could work for both of us. It was understood that, even though the question shouldn't have been asked, it wasn't posed with malice.

Instead, it stemmed from a genuine interest in how I managed to "do it all," which is pretty consistent with the unconscious bias often associated with working mothers.

The call concluded with a job offer, and in just a few months, I found myself co-chairing the women's employee action group, organising International Women's Day events, and becoming an advocate for addressing bias while lending a voice to those who hadn't yet found their own. This is just one of the stories from my journey since becoming a working mum.

So how did I end up here? Let's rewind a bit. I had spent the previous 15 years working for another Big Four bank. After giving birth to my beautiful twins seven and a half weeks prematurely and navigating one of the most challenging years of my life, including being a NICU parent for a month and working through PTSD and PND (stories for another time!), I returned to work in late 2018. I was working through the teething issues—literally and figuratively—of being a new working mum, and after adjusting to my new normal for around six months, I learned that my role was being retrenched.

I didn't see that coming. And it was somewhat ironic. As a 'Type A' personality and self-confessed 'recovering perfectionist,' I had spent a significant part of the previous 5-10 years of my career looking for a role that would allow me to return to work after having a family and "do it all." I was a planner, and I had planned it all! Until we accidentally fell pregnant... with twins!

Working in a male-dominated industry there were very few women around me at that time who had demonstrated that it was possible to have a successful career and raise a family. Most of the women I had as role models had full-time support at home for their growing families, didn't have a family, had older or less dependent children, or worked part-time, often in the retail sector, which had better flexibility in part-time, casual, and school-hour roles. I couldn't see how it would work for a full-time mid-career woman with a partner who also worked full-time.

To plan for "doing it all," I had put myself into a role that I thought I could come back to in a flexible capacity. In doing so, I had given up some opportunities along the way to make those mid-career leaps, including relocations and the chance to live in different states. I felt it would have been too risky since I hadn't seen how other women could do the roles I aspired to do while also having a family.

If I could go back to the time before having kids, I wouldn't let planning for what I *might* need in the future hold me back from doing the things I wanted in my career and in life. Who knows when you might start a family, or if it will happen at all, and even if it does, even with perfect planning, you can't control everything. You may find yourself unexpectedly retrenched and back at square one with a couple of babies in tow—the irony!

I grew a lot in my first year as a mum; the term "matresence" (google it!) is a good way to describe it. Between the hormones, the sleep deprivation, the complete 180-degree shift in routines and structures I used to have, and the changes in relationships and values, I emerged as a different person. I realised that I was planning for a future version of me who I thought would be the same, but post-kids, I was fundamentally different.

Becoming a mum forced me to step out of my comfort zone, to take on projects I had no skills or experience in, to work through hard (and sometimes scary) emotions, to manage insane logistics, and to do it all with no one over my shoulder giving me feedback or praise. And all of this on minimal sleep and the subsequent crushing exhaustion and fatigue that comes with it. Oh, and two small lives (literally) depended on it. It forced me to look inside of myself like nothing before, and I realised I was incredibly resourceful, agile, resilient, compassionate, and vulnerable all at the same time. This new person was definitely not going to be the same worker she was before having a family.

Returning to work for mums postpartum can be one of the most vulnerable times in their careers. You're a new person, navigating new values, and experiencing intense emotions related to leaving your kids in childcare to work in a job that may no longer hold the same passion for you. For me, this was a lot to handle. To add to that, when daycare is involved, kids pretty much catch every bug under the sun. In the first 12 months of daycare, we had cases of slap-cheek, every possible ear infection, three out of the four versions of hand, foot, and mouth disease, a bout of family gastro (which I do not recommend), and all the usual colds and flus. In a month, we'd have about one week of recovery before the next round of infections made its way through the family.

I had also learned a few lessons in my first nine months back in the workforce, including my decision to never work 0.80 FTE or in a 4-day part-time role ever again (I produced the same outcomes as my full-time peers and took on additional projects for the privilege of being paid 20% less). Navigating the first year of work and childcare is a rollercoaster, to put it mildly.

On top of all of this, I felt the pull between wanting to prove I was still a great and committed worker like I used to be before kids (aka work as if you don't have a family) but also be there for my family (aka parent like you don't have a job). The expectations to navigate work, family, and societal pressures at a time when you are already grappling with self-identity can be A LOT!

Soon, I learned that I couldn't do it all without risking serious burnout. I needed to realign my high expectations to match reality. This involved learning to outsource and automate as much as possible. For us, it meant hiring a cleaner once a fortnight, using a meal delivery service, setting bills on autopay, scheduling dog food delivery, and doing a lot of online shopping. It also meant prioritising 'done' over 'perfect' and letting go of the perfectionistic personality traits I had carried for so long.

My husband and I also manage our household as another entity for which we share responsibility. We have Sunday night run-throughs to plan the week ahead and figure out each person's schedule and any deviations from the regular routine. It's been a continuous process of adaptation where we've both needed to be flexible while recognising our priorities for work and home. It's about being so organised that you can adapt to disorganisation at the drop of a hat and still make it work.

Now, where was I? Six months after returning to work after maternity leave, my role was retrenched. Initially I thought it would be fine. I'd had 15 years with the company, had worked across most segments in banking, was well-networked, and had just proven to myself that I could do whatever I put my mind to. However, I had forgotten that almost my entire network consisted of people from the banking industry, and I was now a mother of very young dependent children, which meant I had significant commitments outside of work. I was a new woman, a new mother, and unemployed for the first time in my life. Yikes.

During my period of unemployment, I encountered a great deal of unconscious bias while networking and job searching. I found myself trying to change to fit employers' expectations of full-time work. I initially thought that I was the issue that needed to change. However, it became clear that it's not the individual who needs to change, but rather the system that requires transformation. To contribute to this change, I realised that I must advocate for myself and others and challenge the status quo.

Utilising the lessons I learned from stepping outside my comfort zone as a new mum, I decided to be more intentional in my networking efforts. I found that by strategically choosing the groups I engaged with and by being a human rather than just a job title, I was able to meet some amazing people, including other mums making it work in different industries. It opened my mind to the possibility that "having it all" didn't necessarily have to be the exhausting and unattainable externalised ideal; it could actually be something that works for me and my family.

In 2022, I made the transition to another Big Four bank to find a better cultural fit and an environment designed for success, where employees are valued not only for the work they produce but also for their holistic selves, regardless of the life stage they are in. While we, as a society, still have a long way to go in addressing gender bias in the workforce, there are companies that genuinely prioritise the well-being of their employees. They understand that working mothers bring a wealth of experience, empathy, understanding, and knowledge to the workplace, making them highly desirable contributors.

The struggle of being a working mum is real, but with the right strategies in place, it can become much easier. Here are some things my husband and I have done to make it work along the way:

Learn to ask for help.

Round up the parents, babysitters, friends, and family! With twins, especially in the early years, the logistics of seeking help meant we needed to enlist two people. Humans aren't really designed to handle this on our own, and we need to build villages.

Our village is still growing and has evolved over time. When I first returned to work, our kids spent two days in daycare, one day with hubby, one day with me, and another day with my parents each week, which helped us get through those first few years.

After that, we transitioned to a kindy roster with a 5-day fortnight and school hours. We needed this for a year just to get through, knowing it wouldn't be a permanent structure for the kids or us. Hubby continued with his compacted week, and I worked on a flexible fortnightly roster.

Now that the twins are in school, we arrange after-school care for a few days each week, my in-laws help out for one afternoon, and hubby and I flexibly manage drop-offs and pick-ups. It's not perfect yet, but then again, nothing ever is. We take each week as it comes and adjust accordingly. We're also learning how to navigate school holidays, and taking advantage of my work's option to purchase leave has been a lifesaver.

Flexibility is a need, not a want.

There is a lot of information available about the benefits of flexibility, and I strongly believe that flexible working options should be available (where practicable) to all individuals, regardless of their gender, age, or parental and caring responsibilities.

My husband still maintains a compacted week over four days (yes, he was doing it before it was trendy!), and my roster remains flexible, adjusting to our business and family needs. I'd love to see more men embracing flexible work options and advocating for their necessities. We couldn't successfully pursue our careers and raise kind, resilient, bright, and funny little humans without both of us having access to these options.

Set boundaries.

For me, at work, boundaries look like starting something the same way I intend for it to continue. When I started at the Big Four bank after the retrenchment, I felt the need to make up for being a mum and to try to catch up on the 15 years of impact I had at my previous company, and I went too hard too soon. I was trying to separate work and home, but the reality is that they are a combined beast and need to be managed as such.

When I started in my current role, I was very clear about when I was and wasn't going to be available, was open about the fact that I have a young family but can also do my job if I manage all things well, and I am open with my management and team when things aren't working on either side.

I no longer pretend I don't have a family because I want the younger generation to be able to see a career woman with small kids "doing it" (which I didn't see), and the realities of that mean that I'm not available to do nights on the regular, I may leave functions before 9:00pm because sleep is important to me, and there are times that little people will ask for snacks when I'm on the phone to a colleague.

I don't want to pretend it's all roses and sunshine because it's not; but it is possible when you set clear boundaries in line with your values and give yourself grace when you don't get it right (which happens often!).

There is no such thing as "doing it all."

Working mums are not superheroes, and we're tired of pretending to be. I regularly feel like I've failed at work and at home, and usually on the same day.

I'm often tired, but I turn up to work 'on' and ready to be my best self. I try not to carry around mum-guilt when my child is pulled off me at drop-off because they want to stay with me, or when I have to work late or attend work events making me miss bedtime stories and cuddles. Some days I miss gym workouts, and I often prioritise sleep.

It's hard to show cracks and be vulnerable about the realities of being a working parent, but I want to role model the human parts of being a working mum and not try to be a superhuman because it's unattainable and exhausting. There is always more on that never-ending list of things you "could be doing."

I like to believe that in managing work and life the way we do, my husband and I are showing our kids what family teamwork looks like. I hope we are teaching them resilience and work ethic, and that they eventually learn that we are people outside of being parents, and know that they are loved, admired, respected, and mean everything to us. So much so that they've made us both become better people who want to help change the world in any small way we can.

In the meantime, we are supporting ourselves financially to give our kids a better financial future in a world that is hopefully much better adjusted to work/life integration than the one we're currently navigating through.

I'm incredibly proud of the little humans we're raising and the way we're often challenging the status quo to help change the world for them, and I believe that taking small steps often is how we continue to head in the right direction.

FIONA YUE

❝ MY ADVICE TO OTHER WORKING MOTHERS IS TO DISCOVER YOUR TRUE SELF. FIND OUT WHO YOU ARE AND WHO YOU WANT TO BECOME, THEN WORK DILIGENTLY TO BE THE ROLE MODEL YOU WANT YOUR CHILDREN TO EMULATE. ❞

Fiona, originally from China, transitioned from a primitive lifestyle to becoming a highly successful entrepreneur. Over the past 20 years, Fiona has served as a university lecturer and has founded, co-founded, and managed businesses across various sectors, including financial institutions, consulting, manufacturing, retail, wholesale, and international trading. These businesses have achieved turnovers of up to $200 million and employed approximately 10,000 people. Fiona credits a change in her mindset for the rapid growth of her businesses and now supports organisations and individuals in embarking on the same journey she has experienced.

FIONA YUE

AUTHOR NAME: FIONA YUE
BUSINESS NAME: PGY CONSULTANTS & MERINO AND CO
POSITION : FOUNDER | DIRECTOR OF BOTH
BUSINESS INDUSTRY: MINDSET CONSULTING | WOOL MANUFACTURER.
WEBSITE: WWW.PGYCONSULTANTS.COM.AU
LINKEDIN: LINKEDIN.COM/IN/FIONA-YUE-0255943B/

I was born in a remote village in Mongolia, China. My childhood was very different from what most people in Australia experience. It was filled with poverty. Everywhere I looked, it was barren—no trees, no water, no colour, frequent sandstorms, and an enormous freezer with nothing to put in it.

When my parents got married, they borrowed $10 from my grandparents. It took them almost 10 years to repay their debt. Yes, we were that poor. While the extreme poverty was tough, it was made a lot easier with the kindness and generosity of my parents.

I was the third daughter in a family of four. We were deeply loved by our parents, who always wanted us to achieve more than what they were able to. They didn't want us to experience the same struggles they did and constantly encouraged us to study and pursue our dreams. My mum is completely illiterate and, to this day, has never set foot inside a school. My dad was fortunate enough to attend school until he was six years old before he had to help with the family business.

Growing up, I was always determined to provide more for my own children just like my parents had done for us. I wanted to ensure they wouldn't have to experience the poverty I did during my own upbringing. And I worked hard to make that happen.

At 18 years of age, having never seen an indoor toilet, never brushed my teeth, and rarely having water to bathe, I had the opportunity to study in Australia. This was one of those opportunities I had been waiting for. With a passion to see the world, I took my very first plane ride to Perth, Australia. Hard work pays off.

When I arrived, I could barely speak English. This was just one of the many challenges I had to overcome. I needed two references to secure any form of accommodation, yet I had never lived away from home. I didn't have any family, friends, or knowledge of the language. The obstacles felt endless. Looking back, I am so proud that I had the tenacity to push through, step out of my comfort zone, and persevere even when it got tough, really tough. This is something I often tell my children, so they understand what is possible in life and what they can achieve if they push themselves.

After completing my MBA (Master of Business Administration), I decided I wanted to run my own businesses. I wanted to follow what I felt was right and was often guided by advice from others. Since then, over the past 20 years I have worked as a university lecturer and founded, co-founded, and managed businesses in various sectors, including financial institutions, consulting, manufacturing, retail, wholesale, and international trading. These businesses had turnovers of up to $200 million and employed approximately 10,000 people.

When my two beautiful girls came into the world, my mother told me about her natural births with no drugs. Despite having more resources and opportunities than she did, I chose to follow the same path. During both births, I endured over 20 hours of labour, feeling as if every bone in my body was breaking. Painful doesn't even begin to describe it, but I successfully had two drug-free, natural births. This experience was another stepping stone in my journey of tenacity and determination that forged my path as a successful entrepreneur.

I didn't take time off after I had both of my children. Once I recovered from the birth, I was quickly back into working seven days a week. It was at a time where I was still very much needed in my business and just didn't have the opportunity to take time off. Our girls went to daycare from a very early age, and it just became the norm.

This definitely wasn't a time in my life when I was calm and happy. I was working so much and trying to raise two babies who were just two years apart. I was stressed, overwhelmed, and absolutely exhausted. Completing an MBA is one thing, but learning how to run a business is another. I definitely wished I had a mentor or someone to guide me through those times.

I always wanted more for my girls, aiming to provide them with the best opportunities in life and shield them from the kind of struggles I experienced during my own childhood. When they were little, I set my mind on sending them to a prestigious private all-girls school in Perth. And I worked hard to make that happen. At the time, the school was a 40-minute drive from our home, and I would drive them there, return to work (near our home), and then pick them up again, every day. Their school was situated by the river, and I would often gaze at the houses, especially this one in particular that had a white chimney and overlooked the river. Whenever I dropped the girls off, I would pause for a moment and dream about living in a house like that. "One day," I told myself, "I will have that view." You know what? Today, one of those very houses is my home.

Knowing that I wanted more set me on a constant search for personal and professional development. When the girls were about eight and 11, I hit the jackpot and my world started to change. I came across Bob Proctor, a self-help author, lecturer, and mindset coach. I joined his program and learned about my mindset and my paradigms—the things that had been holding me back for years. I learned how to work smarter rather than harder and see the positives in the struggles. I will be forever grateful for that journey.

By that time, my husband and I started Merino & Co., a wool knitwear and clothing brand. It was going well, but I was still working long, hard hours. My life changed so much; it was like night and day. It took a lot of work and persistence, but I began to see results. The exact results I had only ever dreamt of. The business started to skyrocket, and I was able to work less and less. That was until COVID struck. Overnight, we lost millions of dollars, and we realised our business model needed to change.

Then, with my understanding of how mindset works, thanks to Bob, we were able to quickly turn everything around. We started to look at the positives and everything shifted. There were opportunities available for the business that we had never even considered. We were able to see things in a new way and from a different perspective, opening a whole new avenue for our business. We got right back on track and started to grow our business in another direction. If I hadn't done the work on my mindset and understood how to face challenges and obstacles through a particular lens, I would not be where I am today. Thank you, Bob.

The struggles I have been through in life and business made me want to share my journey with as many people as I could. At this point, Merino & Co. was thriving, which allowed me to step back and follow a new direction. I wanted everyone to learn the skills that had helped me create a better life for my family, both personally and professionally. So, in 2018, I started PGY Consultants. I began helping family and friends in China, knowing that many of them had faced similar struggles to what I experienced growing up. I coached them through the same program that had transformed my life completely.

After a while, I decided to expand and create a team here in Perth. I hired some employees and embarked on a journey of discovery within the PGY business. Soon, I realised we needed individuals with a real passion for self-development, those without money boundaries and personal limitations, and those who genuinely loved what we do. I had to restructure the business, and we lost nearly the entire team. Sarah Maconachie (whom you might know as the author of this book) was the one constant who believed in our mission; she walked the walk and talked the talk. We shared the same passions and desires to help others live better lives, and it has been incredibly rewarding to be part of so many other people's journeys. Sarah has played a significant role in shaping the business into what it is today.

Now, I have complete flexibility around when and how I work. My husband and I share parenting duties, which allows me to try and balance work and life as well as I can. I get up at 5:00am and start my morning routine with some time to myself. I spend this time reflecting and garnering positive energy for the day. On the days when I drop off the girls at school, I come into the office afterwards. And if they need picking up, I am more than happy to leave work early. I never miss school activities and my weekends are solely focused on my children and watching their sports.

While I have achieved balance, financial freedom, and flexibility today, there were many challenges along the way. For a period of time, we faced constant financial struggles and emotional pain. We struggled financially for years, working seven days a week, and it felt like we were getting nowhere. When I decided to enrol the girls in a private school, the enrolment fee alone was $4,000. At the time, we had no idea how we were going to afford it, but we made it work. However, it was a constant source of stress that we had to face.

I also wish I had a mentor or coach to guide me through my business endeavours and to share my challenges with. I now know just how essential it is to have several mentors/coaches that you can turn to when you need help and support.

Surrounding yourself with these people will help guide your aspirations, inspire you, provide direction, and assist you on your journey by utilising the knowledge they have gained from their own experiences. Not only do these individuals offer you optimism by demonstrating that if they can achieve their goals, so can you, but they also think at a higher level. They will understand your goals and visions because they have already achieved them. It's crucial to surround ourselves with people like this.

My advice to other working mothers is to discover your true self. Find out who you are and who you want to become, then work diligently to be the role model you want your children to emulate. When you understand your mind, you begin to unravel your inner thoughts and feelings, providing you with an incredible opportunity to shape the person you aspire to be. Working on yourself is the best thing you can do for your children, too. It allows you to break down your own barriers and prevent passing them on to your children.

KATE O'HARA

❝ IF YOU ARE NOT HAPPY, YOU'RE NOT GOING TO HAVE HAPPY CHILDREN— THAT'S THE BIG TIP! ❞

Kate has a wealth of business and leadership experience. Her background is in property and residential strategic marketing, digital strategy, communications planning, media planning, community creation and place making across a broad range of sectors including asset development and management (residential, retail, commercial, hospitality), residential housing, the resource sector, banking and education. Bringing decades of branding and PR communications strategy, community development and place making, philanthropy and sponsorship strategy experience, Kate is instrumental in continuing to position Foodbank WA as the leading food relief charity and building our connection with the community as well as charity and corporate partners. Kate is also a Non-Executive Director and been on business and not for profit boards covering the arts, education, sports and business groups.

KATE O'HARA

NAME: KATE O'HARA
ROLE: CEO
ORGANISATION: FOODBANK
LINKEDIN: LINKEDIN.COM/IN/KATE-O-HARA-11366112

SARAH:
Can you tell me a little bit about how you were raised and your family dynamics?

KATE:
I'm one of seven children and was raised in the hills of Western Australia. I'm number six out of seven, and I'm a twin. My twin is a brother, which is, you know, all great fun to grow up with. We went to local Catholic schools, as one does up that way. Being child number six, there was a legacy of children that went before us. My school was a real community school—nothing over the top. Dad was a pharmacist and owned the local pharmacy and liked to be a part of the community. His community interests were diverse and over the years included being a Catenian, a member of Knights of the Southern Cross, was President of the local Shire for a number of years, was on the council, and was a Justice of the Peace. Mum was a nurse and, in the second half of her career, became a matron of nursing homes. So yeah, we grew up in a big, busy house that was just a big rambling place up in the hills.

SARAH:

Did your mum work pretty much throughout your childhood as well? And do you think that shaped the way that you were and your expectations when you had your own children?

KATE:

Absolutely. Yeah. We were all very clearly told to be our own people, have our own lives, and every single one of us did travel after high school before starting our careers. It was a very big thing to go and travel the world. So much so that one of them just didn't come back. She stayed there. We were all, you know, very independent because there were seven of us. My oldest two siblings always say they raised us little ones. But it was just the done thing. You got your own lunch, you sorted yourself out in the mornings before school, and you got yourself down to the bus stop. There was no helicopter parenting. No. You were pretty independent from a young age. And if you chose not to come in and get yourself some lunch on the weekend or on school holidays, well, tough. Do what you like. And we were on a big block, so there was lots to explore and lots of things to do. Lots of freedom.

SARAH:

Can you tell me about your career a little bit before you had children.

KATE:

I graduated from university in the '80s. I was in the era of UWA Commerce graduates when that degree pretty much guaranteed you a job; however, two of us in my year didn't manage to do so. We were all interviewed by various accounting firms and banks, among others. I had been in England before all the interviews, and I came back with purple plaits/dreadlocks, which didn't go down well. So, out of the UWA year, myself and another guy didn't find work, and we were somewhat depressed about that. I got my hair cut short and started working in waitressing. In the early part of the following year, a friend recommended the ad agency Marketforce to me. It was the direct marketing team at Marketforce, which was quite a big deal in the '80s. I wrote them a letter presenting my profile and why they should hire me, and they did. So yeah, that was it!

SARAH:
And where were you just before you had your children?

KATE:
I'd been in Singapore. I started my working career in Australia at Marketforce in '87, and then in 1990 there was an opportunity to work at an agency in Singapore, Daly Naidu Chan (DNC). So, I went up there with two weeks' notice... Oops to the boyfriend! Oh well. And I just moved up there with the full support of my family thinking this is a good thing to do. I was 24 and had a great time! So, I landed, got settled, and got stuck into work. I ended up staying there for four and a half years and came back with a husband and about eight months pregnant!

SARAH:
How fabulous! Did you come back and leave your job, or did you come back with the intention of going back to work in Singapore?

KATE:
I came back to Australia with the intention of having some time as a mother with my child, but my son was nine weeks old when I got a job offer. I had realised fairly quickly that my husband wasn't going to find work easily as he was new to Perth and didn't have networks. So, we moved into the granny flat at my parent's house. We had accommodation with that support, and I could get a job. I saw one job at the Shorter Group, applied for it, got the job, and started working when my son was nine weeks old.

SARAH:

Wow. So, how did you balance that with your husband?

KATE:

We were up in Kalamunda, so yeah, it was a long way down to the office in West Perth. There were a lot of breast pads and a lot of hand pumping! I did the drive for a while, but then we got a rental in North Perth which was much closer. My partner then got a job, and we just moved on to having nannies. So, we had daycare and nannies. On my lunch break I'd go from the West Perth office to the daycare facility in Northbridge so I could breastfeed. Often at work if someone mentioned "baby" or "cry" it would kick off lactation, and I'd have to go and get another jacket or change tops or whatever.

SARAH:

Haha! And in that time, how was that received by the organisation? Were they okay with you going out to breastfeed and stuff like that, or was it a bit of an issue?

KATE:

Well, I was working for Deborah and Bruce Shorter. Deborah is, and was, quite a powerhouse as a female leader. She was all about results, and that's what we were achieving. We were getting results, so she was very flexible, and they accommodated my situation. When I was then able to, and I was earning more, I hired a nanny. Nannies were a significant part of our life. I got divorced when my son was five and my daughter was two and a half, so I just had to have nannies from there on in!

SARAH:

What would you say your biggest challenges were?

KATE:

Well, there's a lot to do. You've got a baby, housework... We also went through eight moves of homes in five years, so that was a challenge! It was just busy, but I always made sure that when I got home, the time I had with the kids was always positive time. It wasn't stressing and getting grumpy about eating dinner or chasing homework. It was always quality time.

SARAH:
I came to hear you speak once, you were talking about your different banks, which I really loved. Can you please expand on that?

KATE:
So, the whole idea is that you can't do everything all the time, and that became very clear to me while I was trying to balance everything, right? It was about 15 years ago when I had to go and speak at a female legal network event, and I'd spoken to the lady who had told me to speak about anything. So, I sat back, and I just reflected. The reality is, in anything in life, if you put time and energy into it, it will flourish. You put time and energy into whichever part of your life, and things will happen. But you can't do it all at once.

Once I got home, that was family time and kid's time. I'd invest in them, and if it was 9:00pm and the kids were still sort of grumbling, I'd still sit there and read. It was their time. That's when I realised, well, that's what happens in a bank. But what became very, very clear, particularly post-divorce, was that the only person who can make you happy is yourself.

And if you're trying to be a super mum and a super boss and super everything, it's never going to work. So, you have to make time for your own happiness and invest in your own happiness. Now whether that's a date night with a partner or a massage, do whatever it is that fills your soul.

So, you have to have your 'happy bank', and you need to treat it seriously. Nowadays, I just like to have a walk. I'll take the dog out or whatever, to make sure I've got space and fresh air because that makes me happy and it fills that bank.

I also realised outside of the 'happy bank', you need to have a network, and particularly in Perth. It moves on the wheels of who you know, so I always made sure I invested in my network, so that's my 'social bank'. It became very clear that your network and your friends are actually going to be around longer than some of your marriages. I was very, very invested in board roles and professional programs and networks. It's so important to build that goodwill that you need on your own path. But it was really important to me to not forget that the education side of things and professional development were needed more than just a friendly chat. You need another extension to your skillset and stretch your capability. Now that might be reading books on meditation or something, but you should always strive to improve your mind. And while appreciating that money is needed to keep a household going, it's not the only thing. Personal happiness is vital. As are professional networks and having those people you can turn to for support and keeping your mind activated are all really important, but you have to know what your focus is on at any one time.

And you also have your 'body bank', your fitness. Get some exercise in. I've always had cross trainers and rowing machines, and all the rest of it, and they're really important to have. I'm not obsessed with it, but you've got to have your balance at your bank. You've got to have a balance. You do.

Finally, you have the 'family bank'. Looking after those you love. And at times you have to make a tough call. Sometimes you need to ask them to be patient as you get through the next two months of work because of a deadline or whatever. Or if you are chasing an opportunity that needs more attention.

SARAH:

I love the 'banks' concept! And did you ever get a sense of guilt or anything like that around what you did as a working mum? Or were you pretty confident that it was the right thing for you and your own happiness and your mental health?

KATE:
Oh, look, the one thing I knew was I wasn't going to stay in that marriage, so I had to stand on my own two feet.

I really enjoyed work, and I really enjoyed the people I was working with, so I really got a lot out of that working environment, the friendships, and the networks. I got a lot of support.

Financially, I had to work for the sake of the kids and to get that stability. And as much as the kids will say we've all done therapy and they'll do the whole, "you were never there," you know, work was very important for all of us. I was grateful to have a network to be able to rely on and to be able to balance myself out when the kids were frustrating me. For me, I found work a bit of an escape from the mayhem at times, which I feel like anyone probably does.

SARAH:
Have you noticed a difference within the workplace from when you had children to now and how you accommodate as a CEO within your business?

KATE:
Oh, significantly different. I used to have 7:30am start time for meetings or, on a good day, an 8:00am meeting, and the meeting would've started bang on with all men in the room. I'd walk in at 8:03 or 7:38 or whatever, and they'd go, "oh, nice for you to join us." I lost it one day and said, "I'm really sorry I'm late. But I have got two children to school, one of whom threw their breakfast all over the floor. I've had to do my hair, makeup, and get dressed. I had to re-shower because part of the cereal ended up all over my legs, drive the kids to pre-school care to have them cry at me

while I'm pulling away, and I'm still only eight minutes late. Has anyone else had to do that? Exactly. Good."

SARAH:

I love the fact that you had a voice at that time because it would've been very different to how it is now, and even now, I think that a lot of women are still lacking in the ability to actually have the confidence to speak up when they're being questioned around family.

KATE:

Oh, I fully expected to be walked out of the building. And these days, we can't operate like that thankfully. We've got to actually stop and listen for a minute. I think COVID has helped us all re-think a few things in so many ways. Prior to COVID there was a whole heap of 1990s style management, that meant if you weren't under their nose, you weren't doing the work. And COVID has absolutely forced many to change their thinking. And so that has been a great godsend to working women.

As part of the management team in the agency world, I often supported females to work four days a week. I knew they would work extra efficiently and be a much better operator than someone else who was the preferred candidate who was less experienced and more expensive with little gratitude for the role they're about to be offered. So, I supported giving roles to women. I'd share comments like, "I know she's got three children, but I've worked with her before. Children help make you focussed and effective." It paid off every single time.

SARAH:

And what do you do as a CEO now at FoodBank? What do you do to allow that flexibility within your organisation now?

KATE:

We already have flexibility to work from home for every role that is able to. I mean, I can't do that for a forklift driver, but most of the roles allow for that flexibility. We also have a number of roles that are four days a week or a nine-day fortnight. When I'm looking at what's what, it comes down to the outputs, not the hours worked. And I think that's the difference. It's more about looking at the outputs than the actual situation, which is where a change needs to happen. I think, for working mothers in particular, it doesn't matter what you do for work; if you're doing your job and the outputs are there, then go you!

There's a cultural component as well. Parents are often more effective as part of workplace culture development in an appropriate way. It's that whole reality for a parent that you are no longer at the centre of your own universe, because you've had to raise a child. People change phenomenally after children. It makes you a better contributor and a group member. You become more patient, resilient, and compassionate. So, they're very important. It's essential in workplace culture to have a consideration of presence for that culture development. And we've all seen it in all workplaces. You know, lots of single, young people can all have a great time and all the rest of it, but let's be honest, there is a whole heap of people in their early careers that you don't want to have for long periods of time because you want them to go on and develop elsewhere and grow and come back to you later. When you've had life experience and you build an alumni, and you can create a network of people who can return as experts. It is really good to have young people, but maturity can lead to a healthier culture setting.

SARAH:
If you were to give any advice to other mothers out there, what would it be?

KATE:

Oh, you just can't do it all—you can't do it all, all the time. But you can do it all if you check and balance. It's about knowing yourself well enough. Take time to breathe and take breaks. You know, if you're working and you've got four weeks leave, do the long weekends on a regular basis so that you can get time. Even if it's a Monday off every now and then to do nothing but go to the day spa, or just be in your pyjamas all day, whatever it is that is going to fill your 'happy bank'. They're very important things and very restorative. You can easily be absorbed as a mother or a parent, and you will be very selfless, but no child is happy if their parent is unhappy. Your children are a reflection of your own mental and emotional state. And not investing in yourself is a massive detriment to your children. I see lots of households where there's a lot of expectation and not enough time on self-care. I always ask parents when they have their first child, "How was sleep last night?" If they say, "Oh, I slept through it!" I'm like, "Good, happy household!" I use it as a very good indicator of how everything is going on in the household. Those things are very important to ensure that you've got a healthy working team. Look for the triggers, although sometimes we don't even search for the triggers in ourselves.

Kids are so important and they need you. Parents should be playing with them and engaging with their mind and development. Parents should enjoy their children and for many the rest will come, you know? So, if you are not happy, you're not going to have happy children—that's the big tip!

I think there's a lot of conversation across the media now about the fact that you can't do it all. There is no superwoman, and we shouldn't expect it.

But, with focus, you can achieve anything. So, whatever's your own pathway, you can get there. But it does take a bit of balancing, or blending, whichever way you want to look at it. You can't do everything, but you can have a pretty good crack at it if it makes you happy.

SANDRA LEE

> I DON'T THINK YOU EVER REALLY FIND THE PERFECT BALANCE AS A WORKING MUM. IF WORK GETS REALLY BUSY, THAT TIME IS TAKEN FROM SOMETHING ELSE, LIKE SPENDING TIME WITH THE KIDS. BUT MAKING SURE YOU DO GIVE THE TIME BACK WHEN YOU CAN—THAT'S THE SECRET.

At 56, Sandra has quietly left a trail of success and positive impact. As a mother of two, she navigated isolated and single parenting while growing multiple businesses. She's guest-presented on Channel 9's Education and Training program, built a home-based business to $6.5 million, co-founded a Concrete Batching company, and co-founded an Ed-Tech company listed on the NYSE at $300m+ value with 1.7 million students and 600+ employees. She also co-founded an Entrepreneur Resort Group in Bali, Europe, Singapore, and South Africa. Sandra's grounded upbringing on a farm in the Central Wheatbelt of WA instilled morals such as treating people equally, practicing gratitude, and giving back. She values keeping it real and making a difference for those who aim to live their best life.

SANDRA LEE

AUTHOR NAME: SANDRA LEE
BUSINESS NAME: THE EMPOWERMENT ADVENTURE
POSITION: CO-FOUNDER
BUSINESS INDUSTRY: ENTREPRENEURSHIP & LEADERSHIP
WEBSITE: WWW.THEEMPOWERMENTADVENTURE.COM
LINKEDIN: LINKEDIN.COM/IN/SANDRAMORRELL

I was raised by a single mother who was also raised by a single mother. This gave me the double blessing of two incredibly strong role models in my early life. My grandmother single-handedly raised two girls (my mother and my aunt) on a small tailoress wage, and we wore mostly handmade clothes as a result. I remember my sister and I always being dressed in matching outfits—something we recently found photos of and fondly laughed at! When we were really young, we didn't care about these outfits, but as we got older and became more self-conscious, we begged for store bought clothes, or at least different outfits. But looking back, we were always clean, tidy, fed, and looked after with so much love and care. My mum became a single mum when I was seven, and my sister was nine. Mum didn't have a driver's license, and I remember having to walk nearly 2km to the shops with her and help carry the groceries home. From a young age, I needed glasses and regular eye treatments. Mum and I would catch two buses up to the Children's Hospital and have my pupils dilated.

Then because I couldn't see for a few hours, we waited inside until I could handle daylight again to make the two-bus trek home.

It was just the way it was. Money was incredibly tight, but it was never a 'thing'. We lived in a housing commission area and played street cricket with the neighbourhood kids. We walked through a bush track to get to school, and buying lunch was never ever considered or discussed. This lifestyle taught me the value of playing outside and entertaining myself for hours with a few toys or things I made in the garden.

There was a group of girls who used to tease me about this and would throw their leftover lunches or drinks at me. I remember walking home from school one afternoon when I was about seven, and on this particular day those girls escalated to throwing rocks at me. They weren't great shots and most had missed me. But, unfortunately for them, I caught one of the rocks the size of a golf ball and I quickly returned it. It was accurate enough to hit one of the ringleaders right in the middle of her back. Well, all hell broke loose, and she fell down in hysterics, screaming and crying. So, I raced home. Unfortunately, they knew where I lived, and a few hours later there was a knock at the door. The parents of said ringleader were very angry. I was in my room when I heard my parents defending me, saying I would never throw a rock... Whoops! They asked me to come out and confront the girl, who was showing off a very defined red mark on her back. I wanted to tell them that I was actually aiming for her head, but I didn't think it was wise to mention. I admitted what I did, but nobody listened to my defence. I was grounded. Two things stuck with me from that moment: one, always defend your kids in public, and two, listen to them explain the situation. There are always two sides.

As my years continued throughout childhood into adulthood, whenever I did throw a rock—figuratively—I always got caught. Whenever I responded in anger, took a short cut or an 'easy' option, it always backfired. This absolutely shaped me into who I am today. I remind myself to always slow down, especially in situations when I'm not sure what to do, and to take a few extra seconds, or minutes, to make what usually ends up resulting in a better outcome.

When I was nine, Mum married a farmer, and we relocated 2.5 hours away to the Central Wheatbelt in WA. Although we were certainly better off financially—we grew our own fruit and veggies, and we had chickens and sheep—we were far from wealthy. While we lived a frugal life, we never missed out on anything essential.

We spent our holidays camping and travelling around the countryside. Our annual holiday was always an adventure somewhere new, mostly exploring the outback or bush. We made amazing memories, something that has stayed with me into adulthood. We also lived 20 minutes out of town with only ABC TV in the evenings. We had to entertain ourselves, so we built cubbies, worked on the farm, and kept out of Mum's hair.

It never occurred to me not to work after I had kids. I used to say, "Have kids, will travel," meaning that wherever I go or whatever I do, they are coming with me. I used to say this in response to comments from other people—you know the ones. The negative Nancy's who would say, "When you have kids, you won't know what's hit you," and, "Things will never be the same," or my personal favourite, "You won't be able to do anything once you have kids."

I always had the belief that if I had kids, then they were very much wanted, and they would only ever enhance my life. I would never see them as a negative. And I never did. I never considered the option of not having kids—it was always just something I wanted to do. When I was 20, I married a local farmer. A few weeks after we married, we had a surprise pregnancy. We were elated and couldn't wait to share the news with our friends and family! At four months in, complications kicked in and we ended up miscarrying. There was no reason, it was just one of those things that can happen. The doctors said it was safe to try again when we were ready, but as we married young, we made the decision to delay having kids until we were financially set up.

We spent the next six years working hard and saving. I was working full time in a bank and my husband worked seven months out of the year on his family farm. We also bought into a seed cleaning franchise that we ran for five months of the year. This focus set us up with an investment property in Perth and savings to put a deposit down on our own home.

Then we decided it was time to try and fall pregnant. Despite being really busy with work, we felt that the timing was right. We were financially stable, and the franchise was going well. The week before our son, Brodie, was born, I was still working hard in our Franchise Business clocking up 1,500kms driving on my own to and from jobs—something I definitely don't recommend! Brodie ended up coming two weeks early—I am sure—as a result. My husband turned up just as I was giving birth and left straight after to get back to work. A few days afterwards, I drove myself home. I know this isn't everyone's experience, but this wasn't abnormal in those times, especially in the country. I love that fathers today can take time off work and spend this important time with their partners and babies.

It wasn't long after Brodie was born that the local bank called. They were short staffed and in desperate need of some relief work at a nearby branch, even offering me to bring Brodie along. He was only a few months old, and I was still feeding him. He would either be asleep in his pram or be cuddled and adored by my co-workers while I worked my way through the built-up files. As I continued to work at the bank, and as there was no daycare in the area, I was lucky enough to find a more permanent arrangement with a local lady whose kids had grown up, and she looked after Brodie for me on the days I worked.

Truth be told, I never actually had a driving desire to be a career woman. When I was 14, I decided I wanted to become a hairdresser. At 15, I took on a hairdressing job, then reality hit, and I realised it wasn't for me. I turned down my apprenticeship and boarded at a family friend's home in Perth while I completed a 12-month Business Secretarial course, which led me to the bank job when I was 16. The job appealed to me for two main reasons; one was that it was back home in the country, and two, it was a job that just seemed like something I could do.

We decided not to have a big gap between Brodie and his next sibling, so when he was just over two years old, we tried again. Well, we fell pregnant straight away, and nine months later our daughter Tayla was born. We spent the next couple of months packing up our home and moved into a house we had built that was closer to town. Moving closer to town meant we were no longer 35kms away from schools or shops. I could get a cleaner and possibly some babysitting while I worked.

The success of our franchise gave me the confidence to take on the challenge of selling broadacre farm chemicals from our small shed positioned next to our house on our 3.5-acre block. I thought working from home would work well with the kids and have some increased flexibility to my days. As the business grew, I ended up employing a local 15-year-old girl to come and work a few days a week to help with the kids and house while I worked in the office, made sales, and did deliveries. It wasn't long before her hours increased to full-time. Over the next six years, the business ended up growing into one of the largest independent Agricultural suppliers of its type in WA.

I consider myself the organised type. I would make extra evening meals each night and freeze some for when I was out on the road or finished work late. My favourite time-saver was a $25 slow cooker that I used at least once a week all year round, with hot, healthy meals ready to go when we got home late and were tired from work or sport. My other kitchen winning gadget was a Thermomix. This beauty was—and still is—used nearly every day. Blitzing, blending, chopping, cooking… It even produces the odd cocktail as well!

If you were to ask what motivates me, I would say the desire to do everything to a high level. I am a perfectionist and I spend a fair amount of time looking at ways to improve myself or the way I do things. I would spend long drives listening to influential autobiographies or motivational tapes. Years ago, when I upgraded my car, it came with a CD player (yep—that long ago!) and every month I would load six CDs in the player and listen to them as I drove to and from Perth or around the countryside doing deliveries.

The Ag Business I started in the shed gradually replaced my bank salary, and as it grew, I employed two full-time workers, one to focus on sales and deliveries and the other to run the accounts. I was now selling both farm chemicals and fertilisers as well as additional farm supplies. It was turning over $6.5 million in sales, and I had set up a few sub-depots in nearby towns. I also became a qualified forklift instructor and ran forklift training and licensing out of the chemical shed during off-season.

The young girl I had employed was still with me. She was a godsend! She helped out with the kids, some of the household chores, and worked longer hours if the kids were off school sick or on school holidays.

During this time the kid's father and I separated and eventually divorced. When my own parents separated, I remember very distinctly how we were told. I was seven at the time and my sister was nine. Dad took us for a drive and stopped on the side of the road. My sister and I were sitting in the back. Dad turned around, and with little expression, said he had left home, had a new girlfriend, and they had a baby who was already, by then, a few months old. This was our introduction to a new way of life with a surprise half-brother. So, I knew my kids would remember how we told them the news of our split. I organised for us to go to the park with a picnic. They were eight and five at the time. There is no right time to share something like this with your kids, so my focus was to not give them a memory that would 'damage' them.

The divorce took a few years to finalise, and it was messy. My ex moved three hours away, with the kids going down there every second weekend. The six-hour round trip was tiring, but every time they came back home, I made sure I gave them 100% of my focus so they could decompress and adjust.

When Brodie was 11 and Tayla was eight, I was offered a job as State Manager for the fertiliser company I was an agent for. I ended up selling my Ag business and home, and the three of us moved to Perth. It didn't make sense to stay in the country, especially as the only reason I moved there initially was because of my marriage, plus, I wanted to send my kids to a bigger school. When we got to Perth, I got a bank loan and bought a house in the catchment area of one of the best public schools in Perth.

I was always strict on bedtime. When the kids were younger, at 7:00pm I would call out, "toilet, teeth, and bed," and they knew it was time to start winding down and we would have a bedtime story before they went to sleep. In high school it changed to 8:30pm, and then in the later years of their study they had the freedom of going to bed when they were ready. I gave them autonomy over their study and homework times. Early bedtime for the kids saved my sanity! It meant I was able to finish off any work if needed, or just take some down time and recharge.

Both kids were always encouraged to work around the house from a young age, getting stickers added to their fridge chart, and when they had enough stickers, they would get a gold coin. When they got older, around 14 and 12 years old, I would pay them to help me with the business, just small jobs like cleaning the office or coming along to my events and helping with registrations and crewing. They learned how to save money from a young age, and both worked while at high school and university.

I started working for myself again, co-founded an Ed Tech company that recently got listed on the NYSE, and now work as a Board Advisor while also running Women Empowerment Retreats for fun and as a way of giving back. This enables me to continue working from home and remotely, ensuring I have time for my family as they have now grown into independent young adults.

I don't think you ever really find the perfect balance as a working mum. If work gets really busy, that time is taken from something else, like spending time with the kids. But making sure you do give the time back when you can—that's the secret. I made sure I prioritised sports days, school assemblies, netball games, karate gradings, and graduations over work. Even leaving an event in Europe a day early so I could be back in time to watch my daughter's netball grand final.

While teaching my kids the importance of work, education, and independence, I also wanted to teach them the importance of a positive mindset. I used to stick motivational quotes in the bathroom and toilet with sayings like, "Stand in your Power," and "I am enough." I figured they had to use the loo multiple times a day—haha! There is no way to be a perfect mum, but a million ways to be a great one. The little things do matter.

If you asked me what my proudest moments in life are, without a doubt it was being blessed with my two amazing children. I have had the gift of sharing their lives and the pleasure of watching them grow up into beautiful, kind, giving, and loving young adults. I love that I get to continue this journey with them while being a working mum.

My final piece of advice to all the working mums out there would be not to be too hard on yourself when you make a mistake. It's going to happen, and many things will not go as planned. But every day is a new one. Wake up, look at the sunrise, and treat it as a new beginning. Tell yourself you did the best you could at the time. Onwards and upwards!

ALICIA WHITE

❝ AS SOMEONE WHO HAS BEEN ON BOTH SIDES OF DEATH AND DANCED WITH THE IDEA OF DEFYING IT, I KNOW ALL TOO WELL THE FRAGILITY OF THE HUMAN EXPERIENCE. TIME, IT SEEMS, IS OUR MOST PRECIOUS ENTITY. ❞

Alicia White, a mother of two boys, is the founder and operator of Action & Emergency Pty Ltd First Aid Training. As a registered paramedic turned stuntwoman, her unique career experiences provide insights like no other when it comes to the prevention and management of illness and injury. Realising that there were limitations to how many people a single set of paramedic hands could help, Alicia soon shifted her focus towards the education space. She now works to create an entire army of first responders within a community, effectively saving more lives.

ALICIA WHITE

AUTHOR NAME: ALICIA WHITE
BUSINESS NAME: ACTION & EMERGENCY PTY LTD
POSITION: FOUNDER
INDUSTRY: FIRST AID TRAINING
WEBSITE: WWW.ACTIONANDEMERGENCY.COM.AU
SOCIALS: INSTAGRAM: @ACTION_AND_EMERGENCY
FACEBOOK: FACEBOOK.COM/ACTIONANDEMERGENCYFIRSTAID
LINKEDIN: LINKEDIN.COM/IN/ALICIA-WHITE-FIRST-AID
YOUTUBE: YOUTUBE.COM/@ACTION_AND_EMERGENCYFIRSTAID

During gestation, it's not until around the six-week mark that sexual differentiation begins. Babies in utero naturally develop characteristics that are physically female until the male hormone (androgen) receptors are activated. So, genetically speaking, you could have the male chromosomes X and Y, but you still begin your journey into this world—along with the rest of humanity—in the female form. In some instances, these receptors are not successfully activated (termed an androgen insensitivity) resulting in a genetically male human exiting the womb looking entirely female.

Being a woman, therefore, is the default setting for humanity.

Growing up as the eldest of four girls, there was enough oestrogen in our house to power a small army of unicorns. Much as you might think it was all about handbags, braiding each other's hair, and adorning nail polish, it was very much the opposite. In our house, only wild and fierce females were produced—emphasis on the wild and the fierce. Puberty meant back-to-back tsunamis of emotion, which my poor mother was left to navigate on her own. I, of course, was the token Tomboy, not because of any underlying androgen insensitivities but rather due to the absence of male role models and probably a subconscious need to fill that void.

The men in our lives, it seemed, were temporary fixtures. When I was seven, our father gave up on being a parent and relocated to the other side of the world. After years of back and forth between continents, our mother soon settled into the idea of rocking the 'single mum' thing. And that she did.

As the sole caregiver, she wasn't able to work full-time until we were all in school. In addition to this, not one cent of child support ever made its way into her bank account to help with our upbringing. Yet, we always had everything we ever needed, and our home was always spotless. I remember at one stage we had plastic garden furniture in our living room instead of a lounge suite, and a clapped-out car that had to be warmed up in the mornings before it was even driveable. Money and energy were instead spent on the important things: our education, our clothing, our meals. Happiness didn't come with a price tag, and we were rich in that regard.

I guess there's no real time for a pity party when you have four little humans depending on you.

I worried for my mum more than a nine-year-old should. Though I wasn't privy to a lot of the turmoil she was experiencing, I was directly affected by the upheaval process. Children are often far more receptive to their environment than they are given credit for. Though she never asked for it, I grew to support her while my sisters were still so young. Later, Mum settled into a relationship with what would be the closest thing I'd ever have to a father. A good man, the classic Aussie bloke—gruff but with a heart of gold.

A few years later, he left too, but not voluntarily. At 56 years of age, he had a massive myocardial infarct, a giant blood clot that lodged in his major arteries, causing a heart attack while he was at work. The only thing that came home that day were his boots. I watched as my mum broke beyond repair. She was alone, again.

Over the next few weeks, she literally faded away, losing 10 kilos off her already slender frame. My sister and I took turns helping look after the little ones, and on occasion found ourselves physically spoon-feeding Mum when she simply forgot to eat. I had never experienced raw grief like this before. Death turns your world upside down in a heartbeat (or rather, the absence of one). And by all accounts, his was potentially preventable. We found dozens of empty blister packs of paracetamol in his car. He was obviously in pain—too stoic to mention the headaches resulting from the high blood pressure leading up to his heart attack. And seeing a GP for a check-up? HAH! Not in a million years.

Those first eight or so years of your life are said to be some of the most influential, setting the groundwork for the adult you will later become. I spent those pivotal years propping up the women in my life because I had seen that we are strongest when we put up a united front. I believe this to be true, even today. Fight for the things you care about. Expect to get knocked down, because you inevitably will. Just make sure you get back up.

Fighting was not foreign to me; I was introduced to a judo mat (tatami) at an early age by my grandfather, a third Dan sensei, and owner of the Wanneroo Judo Club. An ex-army physical education instructor and police officer, he was firm but always fair, and he had a wicked sense of humour. It was the same black humour that later carried me through my career as a paramedic. When I established my voice in the line of duty, it was never a loud one, but it was direct and to the point. It didn't leave space to read between the lines because effective communication is an absolute necessity when managing time-critical incidents.

The problem, of course, arises when this becomes a part of your personality and you bring this characteristic home. "Headstrong," they call it, or "strong-willed." My family refers to it as "no fluff."

Historically, what separates women from men is their softness, in life, in love, in communication, and even in our physical form. What is it exactly that made me want to be a strong, hard woman? What is it that made me crave the same status that the men in my life carried?

At 21 years old, I was one of the youngest recruits on-road when I joined the Western Australian State Ambulance Service. I was in the process of completing my second degree at this point, the first being a BSc in Biomedical Science (with a minor in genetics), and my second being a BSc in Paramedical Science.

By the time I was a fully qualified paramedic at 24, I had experienced sides of humanity that I had never known to exist. I had stared death in the face, held the hands of the elderly, delivered babies, and sat with the broken. It was a privilege to be a paramedic and to serve my community.

The first few years of my working life were rich with experiences. Putting on that green uniform gave me unprecedented access to the best and worst of people, places, and moments that life has to offer.

Eventually, I was being partnered with junior officers, many of whom were males, twice my age. Overwhelmingly, my experience and education counted for nothing when I stood beside an older male in the same uniform. As the senior clinician on the scene, I was often overlooked by patients simply because I was young and female, reinforcing the stereotypes of yesteryear. To be fair, most of this was likely generational bias since the majority of patients we attended to were elderly. But I didn't fight to make my position clear; it would ultimately unfold organically, affording students the chance to learn, to step into their role, and utilise their new skills. And when they looked like a deer caught in the headlights, I would step into view.

Being underestimated is a superpower.... #holdmycoffee

There is a strength that comes from stillness and knowledge gained from quiet observation, a notion ingrained in me from an early age as the "gentle way" in Japanese, a principle associated with Judo.

The best examples of this can be observed during any emergency response.

Have you ever seen a paramedic run?

The answer is irrefutably no. Paramedics work to bring a sense of calm into the room. Often dubbed the (medical) jack of all trades, master of none, I would argue that we excel at two things: CPR and managing a scene. Body language is an effective tool for communication. If you stand tall and proud, that's what the world sees. Walking calmly into chaos works to slow everything down. It helps bystanders (mostly) respond in a way that makes them a more valuable contributor to the scene. Reducing anxieties allows space for rational thought, affording them the clarity to answer questions in a coherent way or write down an accurate medical history on behalf of the patient. They can also become liabilities if we don't effectively manage that sense of panic, for example, if their anxiety isn't managed while driving behind the ambulance when it's travelling to the hospital with the lights and sirens, we could be needing a second ambulance.

From the second we step on the scene, our presence carries more power than our words ever could. All of this comes about because we walk; we don't run.

As someone who has been on both sides of death and danced with the idea of defying it, I know all too well the fragility of the human experience. Time, it seems, is our most precious entity.

My grandfather died when I was 12; he was only 62. I wish we had gotten the time to exchange war stories and relive shared experiences. He was one of the few people in my world who would have understood the reasons behind my decision to later leave the service to chase down a career in stunts.

When people ask how I got into stunts, my go-to response is that I fell into it (stand aside dad jokes, make way for the killer mum-puns!). The question should be WHY the change? I tend to dance around this subject a bit because often it can be too heavy for the seemingly light-hearted question the audience is asking. The honest truth is, I was too young to be a paramedic.

There is an implicit trust that goes hand-in-hand with wearing green. I call it the paramedic's privilege. What other job do you know of where parents literally throw their sick child into a total stranger's arms? If you attend a major incident and happen to be the first crew on the scene, people will physically pull at you in all directions if it means you will help their loved one first. We are a part of people's worst moments, the pivotal points in their lifetime. And for us, it might have only been one of many on that shift alone. But for that person, it might be the single most earth-shattering moment they have ever lived through; it might even change their life forever.

With that comes a certain sense of gravity. And you'd be a fool to think you can ever leave the emergency services emotionally unscathed.

With the age of retirement constantly being extended, I was aware that I would potentially be exposing myself to other people's traumas for the better part of the next 40 years. Most paramedics tend to join the profession later on when they have accumulated a degree of life experience—or rather, resilience. That being the case, they might only have 20 years' worth of exposure, which is effectively half the potential trauma I was signing up for.

And so the concept of leaving a very "adulty" job for a chance to make dreams come to life was effectively my ticket to Neverland. I took leave without pay, left everything and everyone I knew behind, and travelled interstate to start anew—with a fresh set of eyes. I didn't look around and see other people's sadness; I didn't avoid coffee shops that were near all the hangings and car crashes I'd attended; I didn't drive down a road where I witnessed tragedy happen. I felt lighter.

I trained my butt off across multiple disciplines alongside some amazing performers—figuring you needed to train with lions in order to become one. Some things I was particularly good at, others had to work harder at. One of my skills was the ability to take a particularly dirty-looking wreck, appearing as though I'd broken several bones in my body on impact, but then I'd pop up completely uninjured with a great big, cheeky smile on my face. My happy place was wirework and flying. And I was way too comfortable being set on fire.

There's something ridiculous about wrestling with your own survival instincts, though; they are there for a reason, and that reason is self-preservation. Free-falling from great heights triggered this reflex for me. Attach a single rope or wire to me and I'd launch off practically anything, but as soon as I was free-falling from heights, all bets were off. You see, if your take-off point is a few centimetres off target, it translates to metres at the bottom, depending on how high you are. And that could mean missing the mat entirely. In an emergency setting, falls from greater than three metres are clinically significant, and if they don't kill you, they certainly warrant spinal precautions at the very least. I'd seen a man's scalp flap wide open from a fall off a single-story roof, resulting in massive traumatic brain injury. And I was about to do a practice run from four times that height. Gulp. I negotiated with that rational, medical thought all the way through stunts and somehow managed to silence it when they uttered those magic words: 3...2...1... Action! Being a paramedic, I think, had a lot to do with being able to perform under pressure.

Not only do you have to be self-driven, physically fit, and a little bit "ballsy" to be a stunt performer, but you also have to be wildly talented across a number of disciplines and yet still remain humble. You have to accomplish amazing feats, quite literally defy gravity, and tell no one of your achievements.

The film industry's underlying foundations are built on good relationships, and humility plays a big part in this. People trying to crack the industry often call it "cliquey," which I guess it is, but if you are being suspended from a three-story building on a single wire, you'd want to know the rigging guys who are responsible for stopping your head hitting the ground when you drop. Therein lies the similarities across these two very different career paths: trust, timing, and teammates. Both industries rely on someone else to have your back, so to speak. Both require an ability to sometimes communicate without words. Both require the kind of synergy that almost looks choreographed, to predict the gaps and seamlessly fill them. Both need to perform well under pressure.

Both are effectively unsung heroes.

As I entered the next chapter in my life, motherhood, I soon came to realise the cyclical nature of my existence: taking care of the people around me, working hard behind the scenes, and only stepping into view when called upon. In other words, being seen but not heard.

I decided to redefine this concept; I had something important to share.

Any mother on this earth would attest to the fact that having children ignites some instinctual desire to protect and nurture their young. And while I can keep my children safe now, while they are so dependent, I won't always be there. Inevitably, at some stage, they will leave my side.

Since my collective experience quite literally lends itself to matters of life and death, to the prevention and management of injury and illness, I felt compelled to educate others about the importance of having those additional skilled hands available within the community. So, I created my first aid training company, Action & Emergency Pty Ltd, to effectively teach the community to cradle my children in my absence.

The knock-on effect of this is tenfold since it means establishing an entire army of first responders available to take action in an emergency (spot the pun). Learning first aid is the ultimate selfless act—you don't do it for yourself, you do it to protect the people around you. It protects your children as well as mine. It protects your friends and loved ones and buys time until emergency services take over. As our healthcare resources are currently stretched so thin, this help is inevitably taking longer and longer to arrive. Time is tissue. If you could help preserve it, why wouldn't you?

All the lessons I'd learnt in life transcribed directly across to business:

YOU CAN'T FIGHT GENETICS!

Softness is a characteristic female trait, and one that will serve you well when nurturing relationships in business. Be compassionate and lean into that softness. It will make you far more approachable and help develop trust.

When you radiate your passion about a subject, your eyes light up and your body language softens—you smile more! The person you are talking to will naturally develop a sense of empathy and may even start smiling and reflecting that passion back towards you. This is because of an observable characteristic called social mirroring. A simple smile just made you and your brand become more memorable.

BEING UNDERESTIMATED IS A SUPERPOWER.

Quiet observation affords you an opportunity to view the whole scene, rather than just fixating on the most obvious problems. Being too close to a situation or too involved in the action can result in tunnel vision. Broaden your perspective by stepping back from time to time. Onlookers might interpret your reserved nature as inadequacy, but when the timing is right, show 'em who's boss!

WALK, DON'T RUN.

The perception of time speeds up and slows down depending on your sense of urgency. It is an absurd constraint that we place too much emphasis on, planning our meals around it, our sleep cycles, and even our productivity. We mourn the loss of it some days and wish it away the next. But have you ever noticed how the perception of time changes during an emergency? When you are desperately waiting for someone to take a breath or to stop seizing, time slows right down. By contrast, accidents happen in the blink of an eye. Building a business takes time. Rather than setting yourself goals within unrealistic timeframes, use that time to collect your thoughts, plan your actions and proceed into the unknown—the time will pass anyway. Walking casually into the unknown will help you better understand what works and what doesn't. You can make better decisions and change direction more efficiently as required.

Always remember that what you contribute to the world is just as important as the person standing next to you. And never be afraid to be seen *and* heard.

MICHELLE TRAVIS

> ...THE SKILLS WE DEVELOP IN OUR CAREERS MAKE US MORE EFFECTIVE MOMS, AND THE SKILLS WE LEARN AS MOMS MAKE US BETTER WORKPLACE LEADERS.

Michelle Travis is an educator, author, and mom of two teen daughters. She is a Professor of Law and Director of the Work Law and Justice Program at the University of San Francisco School of Law. As a founding member of the Work and Family Researchers Network, Michelle is an antidiscrimination law scholar and an advocate for workplace flexibility. Michelle's recent book, Dads For Daughters, is a guide for #girldads to become stronger advocates for gender equity. Michelle is also the author of an award-winning children's picture book, "My Mom Has Two Jobs", which celebrates working moms.

MICHELLE TRAVIS

AUTHOR NAME: MICHELLE TRAVIS
BUSINESS NAME: UNIVERSITY OF SAN FRANCISCO SCHOOL OF LAW
POSITION: PROFESSOR OF LAW
BUSINESS INDUSTRY: EDUCATION
WEBSITE: WWW.MICHELLETRAVIS.NET & WWW.USFCA.EDU/LAW/FACULTY/MICHELLE-TRAVIS
LINKEDIN: LINKEDIN.COM/IN/MICHELLE-A-TRAVIS

I felt like I had fallen off a cliff and landed in someone else's life. Just a few months earlier, I was a skilled, confident, and highly accomplished professional who had earned tenure at a law school faculty. I wore pressed suits and shiny leather heels. People called me "Professor," invited me to speak at conferences, and sought out my legal insights. But two months into my maternity leave with my firstborn daughter, my prior life was a distant memory. I found myself sitting in a park wearing unwashed sweatpants, sporting unwashed hair, peering nervously at a circle of other moms with their newborns at my first official mothers' group playdate. I was terrified that the other moms would discover that I had no idea what I was doing.

As a former lawyer and current law professor, I knew about the "imposter syndrome" that so many incredibly competent women are made to feel in male-dominated professions. Luckily, I had sufficient privilege, social capital, and wise mentorship that I had largely avoided doubts about my professional legitimacy. So,

I was utterly unprepared for what I experienced when I had my first daughter. Nobody ever told me that you could feel imposter syndrome as a mom.

I loved my daughter with a ferocity that I hadn't known was possible, and I was so grateful to have parental leave to spend with her. I had waited until I was 36 to get pregnant. My husband and I had been married for a decade and had planned for parenthood for a long time. We had worked hard to pay off student loans, get established in our careers, and become financially secure. I was ready, eager, and excited to be a mom. Yet when the time came, I still felt like a fraud.

Ironically, my main research area as a law professor is the intersection between work and family. I write articles, give talks, and teach classes about workplace discrimination against mothers. I have spent years advocating for paid family leave, childcare support, remote work policies, and high-quality part-time and flex-time options. In legal academia, I was known as the expert on "work/family balance," long before I had children of my own. But all of my expertise—along with my lengthy and earnest preparation for motherhood—had just made it more difficult for me to deal with my sense of inadequacy upon my first daughter's arrival.

For any other women who are suffering from imposter syndrome in your motherhood role, please be assured that—just like imposter syndrome in the workplace—your feelings are entirely unrelated to your actual level of competence. Also, be assured that the feeling of "mommy imposter syndrome" will rapidly fade. It was actually quite comical how quickly I went from feeling incompetent to feeling such superior expertise that nobody else could possibly care for my daughter as well as me. The reality is that babies are on an even steeper learning curve than we are, which means you are always ahead of the game. Babies haven't internalized society's expectations of supermoms. Babies are nonjudgmental, have very short memories of your mistakes, and are phenomenally resilient. Most importantly, there are no performance reviews on motherhood.

After having a second daughter shortly after my first, I settled into a work/family routine that I thought was working well. I adored my time with my daughters and reveled in their cuddles, laughter, and curiosity. I was in awe of how they learned at lightning speed. I loved sharing their joy in so many first-time experiences. I found no greater pleasure than reading an enormous stack of books to my daughters at bedtime. I also continued to grow in my career, and I looked forward to each new entering class of prospective lawyers, whose grit and goodwill inspired me every day. With the tenure hurdle behind me, I felt freer to be even more outspoken about the need to redesign workplaces to account for employees' caregiving responsibilities.

Yet despite feeling largely fulfilled as both a mom and a professional, I had the nagging sense that something was amiss. There was a disconnect between the different arenas of my life. It took me a while, but I finally realized that my unease flowed from the fact that I never really brought my full self to either my personal or my professional life. At home, I worked hard to be solely a committed mom; while at my office, I was committed to being solely a legal academic. Looking back, this sustained effort at compartmentalization seems ridiculous, but it was actually quite rational.

As a researcher, I was very familiar with studies finding that when professional women become mothers, their employers and co-workers tend to view them as less competent, less intelligent, and less committed to their jobs. (In contrast, when men become fathers, they are viewed as warmer, but no less career-oriented than before.) I also knew about the gender wage gap and could recite multiple studies on the so-called "motherhood penalty"—the fact that working women's pay and promotion trajectories take a major hit when they become parents. So, it's no wonder that I engaged in secret parenting while navigating my professional sphere by downplaying my motherhood responsibilities whenever I was tending to my work as a professor.

At the same time, I was painfully cognizant of the stigma that also attaches in the opposite direction. I knew about the erroneous assumption that women with career ambitions are less nurturing moms and that their children purportedly suffer as a result. Consciously or not, that knowledge led me to hide my professional responsibilities whenever I was parenting, attending park playdates, or showing up at my kids' school activities.

Although highly rational, the energy required to constantly shift personas took its toll. I felt drained and never quite whole. By constantly focusing "solely" on one role or the other, I always felt like I was missing out on something. This wasn't how I expected "work/family balance" to feel.

Every night before I went to sleep, I found myself assessing my personal "work/family balance" for the day. Had I spent enough time that day as an engaged parent? Had I excelled at today's professional responsibilities? Inevitably, I would find myself cataloguing the undone "to-do" items in both arenas, rather than feeling grateful for the day's highlights. The unread colleague emails outweighed the giggles of my daughters' pajama playtime. The unwashed laundry outweighed the completion of a new lesson plan. There never seemed to be enough hours in the day. My obsession with achieving work/family balance led me to believe that I had spent my professional career advocating for an outcome that I was regularly failing to achieve in my personal life.

I started having an intensely negative reaction to the phrase, "work/family balance." Just hearing the word "balance" flooded me with waves of resentment. Adrift in a sea of working-mom guilt, I serendipitously received a sweet note from my daughter one day. Her note had only two words: "Mom ROCKS." That was my turning point. That's when I realized that I wasn't failing to achieve my goal at all. I had simply set my sights on the wrong goalposts.

The concept of "work/family balance" sets working moms up for failure. "Balance" implies a scale that only allows for direct trade-offs: more weight on the work side necessarily means less weight on the family side, and vice versa. The problem is that on any given day, our time allocation between work and family is virtually never in perfect equipoise. On some days, I left my office early and abandoned an overdue manuscript so I could watch one daughter's dance competition or take my other daughter to the dentist. On other days, I was consumed by grading exams, preparing for a speaking engagement, or reviewing law student admission files, while my daughters ate leftovers in front of the television. On a "balance" measure, it's no surprise that I considered myself a failure at the end of nearly every day.

The concept of "work/family balance" also doesn't fit our lived experience. Work and family are not separated on opposite ends of a fulcrum. Work and family are deeply intertwined. I mentally prepare my next lecture while navigating my car through my kids' school pick-up line. I schedule my daughters' parent-teacher conferences in between advising law students during my office hours. I worry about my kids while attending faculty meetings, and I contemplate how to help my law students better understand the legal rules of negligence while making my kids grilled cheese sandwiches.

Most importantly, the concept of "work/family balance" doesn't capture the powerful synergies between the professional and personal aspects of our lives. "Balance" doesn't recognize that feeling satisfied in our careers makes us more dynamic and creative parents. "Balance" doesn't acknowledge that the skills we develop in our careers make us more effective moms, and the skills we learn as moms make us better workplace leaders. In other words, "balance" ignores that work and family are not a zero-sum game.

My disillusionment with the concept of "work/family balance" ultimately led me to a healthier goal. I now strive towards (and advocate for) a sustainable work/family integration. By seeking work/family "integration" instead of "balance," I've made several important shifts in my perspective, which has helped me recognize that I am actually succeeding beyond my wildest expectations as a working mom.

First, striving for integration allows me to stop taking stock of my time allocation on a daily basis. Instead, I take a far more meaningful, bigger-picture view. At the end of each week, month, or year, can I look back and feel like I've spent enough time with my kids to ensure that they feel safe and loved, that they are kind, joyful, curious, and that they are making friends and excelling in school, and that they are still happy to spend time with me? Can I look back and feel like my law students are thoughtful and committed future lawyers, and that I am making progress (regardless of the pace) in some area of legal research that piques my own curiosity? If the answer to these questions is "yes," that is my success, even if my day-to-day ebbs-and-flows say otherwise. When the goal is "work/family integration", my daily imbalances are no longer a failure, but instead the foundation for a beautifully varied, rich, and satisfying life.

Second, embracing work/family integration empowers me to bring my whole self to both arenas of my life. I make sure that my kids understand why training future lawyers is important work, and they are proud of me, even if that means they spend some evenings in front of the television. I also make sure that my law students know that as a working mom, I respect their own need to attend to family responsibilities as well. Students are welcome to bring their children to my class or seek an assignment extension when caring for a sick family member. My students appreciate my commitment to both career and family, even if it means that I sometimes take a few extra days to grade their exams. When the goal is work/family integration, my inability to compartmentalize work and family is no longer a failure, but a wonderful opportunity to connect, learn, and grow.

Third, focusing on work/family integration liberates me to

stop focusing on my perceived shortcomings as a parent or as a professor, and to instead celebrate the synergies. Having a challenging, impactful, and fulfilling career makes me more enthusiastic, present, and engaged when I am with my kids. My career has also given me a unique perspective on different learning styles, listening techniques, and diverse perspectives, so I am far better equipped to teach my kids the skills, values, and life lessons that I hope to impart.

As a researcher, data is my comfort food. So, for me, data has been the strongest antidote for working mom guilt. I find great solace in studies that validate my sense of the value that working moms bring to their parenting role. Contrary to popular belief, children of working moms do not suffer emotionally or intellectually. In fact, working moms tend to engage in more cognitively stimulating playtime, which is fantastic fuel for their children's developing brains.

Researchers have also found that working moms raise daughters who are more resilient, independent, and have a stronger work ethic. According to a Harvard Business School study, daughters of working moms grow up to have more successful careers of their own and earn significantly more money than girls whose moms did not have paid jobs. Working mothers also raise sons who end up sharing household and childcare responsibilities more evenly with their own partners later in life. Knowing that working moms are helping narrow the gender gap in these important ways made it much easier for me to jettison my insecurities. It turns out that workplace leadership skills—like strategic planning, flexibility, and innovation—are the same skills that make women exceptional parents.

The reverse is also true. My experience as a mom makes me a stronger, more patient, and more tenacious workplace leader. A study from the Rutgers Centre for Women in Business has confirmed what working moms already know: that raising kids and running a family build extraordinary project management, multitasking, and problem-solving skills. There is no doubt that being a mom makes me more efficient with my time, not less.

Motherhood is also an unparalleled leadership training ground. Being a mom requires expertise in people management, conflict resolution, negotiation, collaboration, communication, and team building. Motherhood demands keen observation, active listening, and the ability to mentor and give constructive feedback. Two of the most important skills for today's workplace leaders are empathy and adaptability. Those are also the hallmarks of a dedicated mom.

Of course, the challenge with work/family integration is that there's a fine line between synergy and chaos. Blurred boundaries can be both exhilarating and exhausting. That makes it even more important for working moms to look out for one another. On my part, I have resolved to support other working moms by bringing my full mommy-self to my workplace, and my full professional-self to my home. That is how we will ultimately disrupt the negative working-mom stereotypes—in both our professional and our personal realms.

I also take time to celebrate the joyful moments when my daughters remind me that I do, in fact, ROCK. I felt it every time my older daughter proudly wore her "Girls Rule" t-shirt to kindergarten. I felt it when I heard my younger daughter interject during grace before a meal at her grandparents' house to change the word "amen" to "awomen," just to be fair. I felt it when my now teenage daughters let me belt out the lyrics to "The Man" alongside them at a Taylor Swift concert. There are so many ways that your kids will remind you that you ROCK. Use those moments to embrace the powerful synergies of our complex and gloriously messy lives.

ABOUT SARAH MACONACHIE

WWW.WORKHARDPARENTHARD.COM.AU

Sarah can be described as determined, tenacious, and driven to achieve her goals. From a young age, Sarah had a big vision and significant life goals, as well as a fire in her belly to ensure she always achieved what she set out to do. With her optimistic nature, she has always believed that things will work out, and with an ethos that everything happens for a reason, she believes her life has unfolded just as it was meant to.

Originally from the UK, Sarah graduated with a degree in Psychology and soon decided she wanted to embark on an adventure exploring the world, refusing to settle in a place that didn't feel right. She booked a one-way ticket to Australia and never looked back.

Living in Sydney, Australia, Sarah embarked on a career in Human Resources and Recruitment. When Sarah and her husband decided to move to Perth to start a family and be closer to her husband's family, the world delivered once again. Just a week after her husband was offered a job in Perth, Sarah found out she was expecting her first baby, and her motherhood journey began.

Since returning to work after having children, Sarah recognised the need to "bridge the gap" and create more equality for mothers in the workforce. Sarah hears more and more from women that have taken huge pay cuts, have been demoted, and have had to take junior positions once they become mothers. This bias, whether conscious or subconscious, has fed into societal norms from days gone by that once women become mothers, that is their only role in society.

The feeling that we must sacrifice money or seniority to have the flexibility to be a mother also leaves women feeling unstimulated, lacking in confidence, and with low self-worth. There are women who would love to get back to work but struggle to understand how they could possibly balance their new life of having dependents and a career.

On the other hand, men in the workforce are being told they cannot work flexible hours, facing challenges in balancing their career and supporting their family at home. They fear potential setbacks in promotions and bonuses if they choose to utilise their parental leave or take time off to be with their children.

Sarah's own journey led her to write for various publications on topics related to parenthood, working parents, gender equity, and mindset. Her interest and research have resulted in publications challenging the status quo for working parents, presenting perspectives from both mothers and fathers. This inspiration prompted her to write 'Working Mothers Inspiring Others' and 'Working Dads and Balancing Acts'. The aim of both these books is to normalise the need for balance for parents with careers, to share the mental load of parenting, and to provide support and encouragement to mothers who want to re-enter the workforce.

Sarah's desire to support women through the transition of motherhood is the driving force behind all her endeavours related to parenting, including her own business, Work Hard Parent Hard.

CONCLUSION

"You choose the life you live. If you don't like it, it's on you to change it because no one else is going to do it for you." – Kim Kiyosaki

As we close the incredible chapters in this book, I invite you to reflect on where you are as a mother. Are you currently working? Do you aspire to work? Are you happy with your role as a mother, or do you need something more?

Having the confidence to create change in your life can be daunting, but the change could benefit you and your growing family. Our children are a reflection of us. They are born with a blank slate, and the way they think and behave is influenced by us—their parents—as well as the environment they are in.

Creating a life you love, being passionate about what you do, and spending time with your family is essential for your happiness and the happiness of your children.

We no longer live in a society where women stay at home raising the kids while dads are out at work. More and more women want to return to work, and more dads want to spend time at home. Times are changing, and the amazing mothers in these chapters are challenging previous societal norms. They offer advice and encouragement for working mothers, whether it's full-time work, full-time parenting, or somewhere in between, to be the best version of themselves.

You'll find that understanding your wants and needs as a mother and being confident about them are common themes throughout this book. These chapters also underscore the need for support, both at home and at work, as well as the necessity to normalise the flexibility required in the workforce as we raise our children. Use the worksheets in this book to reflect on what you truly want, what will work for you and your family, and how you can create the life you desire. Anything is possible with the right attitude and determination.

Stand strong, ladies! You are a mother, but you are still YOU—an incredible new version of yourself.

REFECTION

- What was your biggest take away from the Chapters

_____
_____
_____
_____
_____
_____
_____
_____
_____
_____

- Name one thing you are going to implement that you learnt from the Chapters

  _____

  _____

  _____

  _____

- How do you feel about your own balance of working and being a parent?

  _____

  _____

  _____

  _____

  _____

  _____

  _____

  _____

  _____

YOUR PURPOSE

When we have children we go through a huge process of change. Pre children we have a carefree life, a job, time to ourselves, no real commitments. We can do what we want, when we want to.

When we have children our perspectives and priorities make an incredible shift. Our children become our priority and we go through a process of figuring out what our purpose is now, what we want and need in order to make us happy and our children/family happy.

I want you to think about the following questions, and answer them as truthfully as you can.
- Do you enjoy staying home with your children full time or Part time?
- Do you enjoy working?
- Do you feel you need a balance of working and being home with your children? What would that look like?
- When do you have time for yourself? and do you actively book things in for you?
- Are you passionate about what you do?

These questions are so important to think about. We often feel like we have to sacrifice something especially in the early years of being a parent, but compromising on the different areas of your life is a much way to look at it.

Being happy makes for much happier children. So it's time to focus on YOU and what your purpose is, what do you want?

Rate the following areas of your life out of 10 and see where you are compromising on and if you are happy with that.

- Work/ Career
- Parenting
- Social Life
- Relationship
- Time for self
- Holidays/ Travel

HAVE A CLEAR VISION OF WHAT YOU REALLY WANT AND SET A CLEAR GOAL!

Totally relax and let your imagination wonder. Take some time to close your eyes and be at one with your thoughts. Think about your life over the next 12 months. If you had all the resources, time, money and support to live exactly how you want to- what would that look like?

Think about all the different areas of your life. What kind of house do you live in, holidays/ travel, education, relationships, business/career, your finances. Allow your imagination to build a beautiful picture of your ideal life in your mind. Your imagination is your real self- make sure it's what you would really love.

Write down a shopping list of your personal and professional wants as if they are in the present tense.

Write down a list of your personal and professional wants

_____

_____

_____

_____

_____

THINK ABOUT YOUR BELIEFS- THIS IS WHAT YOU ARE TEACHING YOUR CHILDREN EVEN IF YOU DON'T KNOW IT!

FINANCIAL WEALTH
If your income was to stop tomorrow, how long could you sustain your lifestyle?
What is the most you have earned in a 12 month period?
How much would you need to earn to consider yourself wealthy?

BUSINESS/ CAREER
When you wake up in the morning, do you feel excited about what you do?
If you could do anything in your career, what would it be?

HOLIDAYS
How often do you go on holiday? Where do you go? What type of accommodation do you stay in? Are you able to do what you want freely?

HOME
How would you describe the house you live in? Is it in an area you love?

RELATIONSHIPS
How would you describe your relationships with your family and friends?

CHILDREN

Are you happy with the amount of time you spend with your children?

Are their any aspects of your own upbringing that you would like to change in the upbringing of your own children?

Do you understand why your children think and behave the way they do?

How you answered those questions gives a very clear indication of where your paradigms sit. It should have made you think about where you are now, and where you would love to be.

How we think and behave also has a direct reflection on how you are raising your children to think and behave,

When you answered the questions, think about if you want to change, what is the life that you truly want to live?

How do you want your children to be raised to think and behave?

WORK HARD PARENT HARD DAILY SUCCESS GUIDE

1. **Morning Dream Session:** Before you even think about escaping the clutches of your oh-so-comfy bed, keep those peepers shut! Picture your dream life. You know, the one where you're not just scraping Weetabix off the kitchen table but living large and in charge! Feel it – the pride, the joy, the "I've-got-my-life-together" vibes.

2. **2. Gratitude Graffiti:** Now, hop out of bed and jot down 10 things that make you feel grateful. It could be your kiddo's toothless grin, your partner finally remembering to put the toilet seat down, or just the fact that coffee exists. Close your eyes, take a deep breath, and send some cosmic high-fives to the universe. Got someone bugging you? Imagine texting them, "Hey, you're awesome, and I am so grateful you have stopped using my mug."

3. **Ideal You:** Write down your "worthy ideal." Something like, "I'm over the moon that I've finally mastered the art of hiding veggies in meals so my kids eat them." Keep telling yourself this – your subconscious is listening (and it's a better listener than your toddler).

4. **Self Pep-Talk:** Time for your daily affirmation. Try: "I'm an excellent parent. I am great in my career, I spend quality time with my children, and I have the balance of both down pat."

5. **Life Script:** This is your chance to be the scriptwriter of your own blockbuster life. "I always have enough money to buy whatever I want for myself and my family "

6. **Action Hero Mode:** Write down 6 things you will do today. They need to be action points that will help you to reach our overall goal, if it's something someone else could do- remove it from the list immediately!

7. **Priority Juggling:** Throughout the day, tackle things based on how much they'll help you reach your "Goal." Got a problem? Take a deep breath, channel your inner Zen master, and ask, "What would Super Me do?"

8. **Goal Card Gala:** Whip your goal card whenever possible. It's like a backstage pass to your dreams.

9. **Worthy Ideal Check:** Whatever you're doing – conquering the world or just staring into space – ask yourself, "Is this getting me closer to my dream?"

10. **Nighty-Night Manifestation:** Repeat your morning dream session before you hit the hay. The mood you snooze in sets the tone for your morning!

REMEMBER: You are what you think about. Choose those thoughts like you choose your battles – wisely and with a sense of humour! The great thing is you can do all of these while spending time with your little ones. I ask my 4 year old what she is grateful for most days and it's always a beautiful response!

www.ingramcontent.com/pod-product-compliance
Lightning Source LLC
Chambersburg PA
CBHW070546010526
44118CB00012B/1240